10/06

Bloom's
GUIDES

Mark Twain's
The Adventures of Huckleberry Finn

1984
The Adventures of Huckleberry Finn
All the Pretty Horses
Beloved
Brave New World
The Chosen
The Crucible
Cry, the Beloved Country
Death of a Salesman
The Grapes of Wrath
Great Expectations
Hamlet
The Handmaid's Tale
The House on Mango Street
I Know Why the Caged Bird Sings
The Iliad
Lord of the Flies
Macbeth
Maggie: A Girl of the Streets
The Member of the Wedding
Pride and Prejudice
Ragtime
Romeo and Juliet
The Scarlet Letter
Snow Falling on Cedars
A Streetcar Named Desire
The Things They Carried
To Kill a Mockingbird

Bloom's
GUIDES

Mark Twain's
The Adventures of Huckleberry Finn

Edited & with an Introduction
by Harold Bloom

CHELSEA HOUSE
PUBLISHERS
A Haights Cross Communications Company ®
Philadelphia

A Haights Cross Communications ⚡ Company ®

www.chelseahouse.com

Contributing editor: Janyce Marson
Cover design by Takeshi Takahashi
Layout by EJB Publishing Services

Introduction © 2005 by Harold Bloom.

First Printing
1 3 5 7 9 8 6 4 2

Library of Congress Cataloging-in-Publication Data
The adventures of Huckleberry Finn / [edited by] Harold Bloom.
    p. cm. — (Bloom's guides)
  Includes bibliographical references (p.   ).
  ISBN 0-7910-8241-5 (alk. paper)
  1. Twain, Mark, 1835-1910. Adventures of Huckleberry Finn. 2. Finn, Huckleberry (Fictitious character) 3. Mississippi River—In literature. 4. Boys in literature. I. Bloom, Harold. II. Series.
  PS1305.A34 2005
  813'.4—dc22
                                        2005003089

Contents

Introduction

HAROLD BLOOM

For a country obsessed with the image of freedom, Huck Finn is an inevitable hero, since he incarnates the genius of American solitude. Richard Poirier observes that *Adventures of Huckleberry Finn* is marked by the quietness of its autobiographical narrator. Huck talks to us, the readers, but only rarely to the other figures in the book, even to his companion, Jim. Loneliness is the condition of Huck's existence; he belongs neither to the adult world, nor to that world's antechamber in Tom Sawyer's gang. Truly, Huck is as isolated and eccentric a figure as "Walt Whitman," the hero of *Song of Myself*, and Mark Twain, as Poirier remarks, never found a fit context for Huck after the first sixteen chapters of *Adventures*. Partly, this may mean that Huck is larger and more vital than his book, admirable as it is. But I suspect that ultimately Huck stands for what is least sociable in Mark Twain, whose discomfort with American culture was profound. Like Huck. Twain had decided to go to hell, if that was the only way to escape his neighbors and country, and if that was the only path to freedom.

Since Huck is neither a god nor a beast, he suffers intensely from his loneliness. If you define freedom as a relationship within society, then Huck is a negative image only: the hero as misfit. Classic American literature, however, does not easily permit societal definitions of freedom. Hester Prynne in *The Scarlet Letter*, Ishmael in *Moby-Dick*, Thoreau at Walden Pond, Emerson confronting the past: all provide images of isolation as an inner freedom, and the exiles of Henry James have a way of reestablishing their American solitude in centers of sociability like London and Rome. Whitman proclaims the love of brothers while finding his particular metaphor for poetic creativity in Onanism, and Emily Dickinson's self-segregation is notorious. The tradition does not vary that much in the great writers of our century, where our poets remain lonely: Robert Frost. Wallace Stevens, T.S. Eliot, Hart Crane, Elizabeth Bishop, John Ashbery. One thinks of the protagonists of our major novelists: Dreiser's Carrie, Cather's Ántonia, Fitzgerald's Gatsby, Faulkner's Joe Christmas: these also are isolated dreamers. The American religion of self-reliance carries with it the burden that no American feels wholly free until she is truly alone.

Fitzgerald, Hemingway, and Faulkner all exalted *Adventures of Huckleberry Finn*, seeing in it their American starting point. Their tributes were rather fierce: Fitzgerald said that Huck's "eyes were the first eyes that ever looked at us objectively that were not eyes from overseas," while Hemingway placed the book first among all our books, and Faulkner's final novel, *The Reivers*, explicitly presents itself as a revision of Twain's masterpiece. What disconcerts many critics of *Huckleberry Finn*—the slippage between Huck as narrator, lying his way to a kind of freedom, and Huck as active character, ultimately manifesting a generosity of spirit beyond everyone else in the book except Jim—seems not to have bothered Twain's novelist descendants. Twain gave them a fascinating fourteen-year-old quasi-scoundrel in Huck, a trickster as resourceful as Homer's Odysseus or the biblical Jacob. Though Huck may look like an unvarying picaresque hero, he actually is a master of disguises, and he changes incessantly, while growing no older. He is very hard to characterize because he is not still long enough for us to know exactly who he is. Nor is his own sense of identity securely established: he both is and is not his dreadful father's son.

Huck's central freedom is essentially authentic: he always will be fourteen years old, because we cannot envision him, say, at forty. Lighting out for the territory will not age him; whether his morally ambiguous attitude toward society could survive maturation is therefore an inappropriate question. That may be why *Adventures of Huckleberry Finn* ends in a fashion unsatisfactory to nearly every critical reader the book has attracted. We all want Huck to be better and stronger, and even more self-reliant than he is. He has broken with the morality of slaveholding, but the break has ravaged and confused him. We cannot have a politically correct Huck, which is why the book continues to offend so many, who simply do not know enough nineteenth-century American history to see that—for his time, in his place—Huck is a miracle of self-emancipation. Yet he is not only pursued by the murderous Pap Finn; he also carries much of his father within him, as Harold Beaver has shown. *Adventures of Huckleberry Finn* has only a few rivals as the indispensable work of nineteenth-century American literature: *Moby-Dick*, *Leaves of Grass*, *The Scarlet Letter* are among them. Ahab, "Walt Whitman," Hester Prynne all inform our sense of ourselves, but it is primarily in Huck Finn that we study our nostalgias.

Biographical Sketch

Samuel L. Clemens, who in 1864 adopted the nom de plume Mark Twain, was a colorful character who used a broad spectrum of personas in his books, from the carefree young boy rafting on the Mississippi to the Connecticut Yankee exposing the corruption of old European culture. As a young man, Clemens loved to travel to exotic places, indulging an irrepressible spirit of adventure. Later, as an enormously popular author, he became a part of the American mythology he created, a man who spent a lifetime cultivating his public image with the unique brand of humor that he demonstrated in both his writing and his public lecturing.

Edward Wagenknecht says in his biography, *Mark Twain: The Man and His Work*, "The great characters of fiction are built from the inside out.... They are so many emanations of the man who created them; and the life that informs them, as they go about their business in the world, in his life. Only by life can life be created." Twain did exactly that. He used his childhood experiences in Hannibal, Missouri, to weave romantic tales that memorialize a particular place in America at a particular time in history. For all that he turned his childhood memories into mythology, Mark Twain also preserved a social history. His record of his adolescent years is replete with humor, and yet it gives us a searing commentary on the cultural superstitions, racial prejudice, and institutional blindness of America just prior to the Civil War. His stories are always unpretentious, written in the colloquial language of the region. They leave us with an enduring picture of a vanished way of life.

In 1856, at the age of twenty-one, Samuel Clemens's wanderlust increased his desire to get away from his older brother Orion, a journalist and publisher for whom he was working at the time. He dreamed of making his fortune importing coca from the upper Amazon. However, although Sam was lucky enough to find $50 to finance part of his travels, the trip never took place. Instead, he seized another opportunity, satisfying a boyhood dream of becoming a steamboat pilot. He apprenticed himself to Horace Bixby, the pilot of the *Paul Jones*, but his piloting days were not entirely idyllic.

Bixby is said to have questioned Sam's courage as he dealt with the idiosyncrasies of the Mississippi. Sam Clemens had a nervous personality, and no doubt he demonstrated his anxieties on the job. Nonetheless, no serious navigational accidents occurred while he was piloting, and apparently Bixby felt he knew the river well enough that he even took him in as his partner.

The most traumatic experience during Sam's piloting days from 1857 to 1861 was when he witnessed his brother Henry die. Sam had helped Henry get a job on the steamboat *Pennsylvania*, but a few days later, the steamboat blew up near Memphis. Sam sat by Henry's side in a makeshift hospital and watched while he died from his burns.

But for all the trials and tribulations he experienced as a pilot, Sam Clemens described those years as joyous and fulfilling. "Piloting on the Mississippi River was not work to me; it was play—delightful play, vigorous play, adventurous play—and I loved it." Clemens' piloting days on the Mississippi contributed to his literary development by giving him the opportunity to study with a keen and perceptive eye the people who traveled the river and lived along its banks. As he was to write in *Life on the Mississippi*, "In that brief, sharp schooling, I got personally and familiarly acquainted with about all the different types of human nature that are to be found in fiction, biography, or history."

He published two imaginative prose pieces during this time: "River Intelligence," a letter attacking a self-important older pilot; and a spoof on the memoranda pilots wrote for their colleagues, a satirical piece that appeared in the *Missouri Republican* in August 1860. His early writings' blend of fact and fancy provide a glimpse of what was to become an essential part of Twain's future achievement as both a writer and a public speaker. In 1861, however, his piloting days came to an end when the Civil War virtually stopped all commercial river traffic.

Clemens's involvement in the Civil War was very brief. He claimed to have anti-war sympathies, but in April 1861, he went home to Hannibal and joined some of his old friends, Confederate sympathizers who referred to themselves as the "Marion Rangers." Hannibal was controlled by the Union, and thus their activities had to be covert. The "Marion Rangers" were quickly discouraged by the Union presence, and they disbanded before they were ever actively engaged in the war. Wagenknecht points out that what is interesting here is why Clemens got involved with this group in the first place; his actions reveal the ambivalence of the border states. Before Clemens joined the "Marion Rangers," he had voted against secession, since he did not wish to be forced into military service as a military pilot. "I must also say," Wagenknecht writes, "that his whole contemporary Civil War attitude shows little political intelligence. In Virginia City he associated with Union men and 'secesh' men with fine impartiality, and it must have been difficult for anyone to find out where his sympathies lay." (On the other hand, as Wagenknecht states, Clemens' perspective on the Spanish-American War was quite different. He detested the monarchy, and clearly supported the war.)

In the end, Clemens's circumvention of the Civil War opened new horizons of experience that he eventually transferred to his writing. In 1861, he accompanied his brother Orion to the Nevada Territory, beginning his "westward expansion." In his biography of Mark Twain, John C. Gerber states that in the West Clemens decided on his writing profession, and there he adopted his famous pseudonym: Mark Twain, a term from his riverboat days that means "two fathoms deep" or "safe water." "Attempting to win the acclaim of readers in Nevada and California," Gerber writes, "he exaggerated heavily and resorted frequently to burlesque and occasionally even to hoaxes."

His brother Orion made the trip west possible. In 1860 Orion had campaigned for Abraham Lincoln and then had the good fortune to work briefly for the new Attorney General, Edward Bates. As a result of these connections, Orion received a political appointment as secretary for the Territory of Nevada.

The brothers left by steamboat in July 1861 for St. Joseph, Missouri, and arrived in Carson City by stagecoach in August. Although Clemens did not make his fortune in timber or silver mining as he had hoped, his occasional writing of humorous letters, signed "Josh," for publication in the *Territorial Enterprise*, rescued him from any economic difficulty. As a result of these letters, Clemens was offered a job as a local reporter and freelance writer.

This early writing career gave him the opportunity to hone his skills at writing short narrative while exploring a wide range of subjects. Equally important, during these years he also developed friendships with three master storytellers: writer Bret Harte, the professional lecturer Artemuis Ward, and the amateur storyteller Jim Gillis. Clemens's skill as a public lecturer adept at storytelling led to his early critical acclaim. During his time at the *Territorial Enterprise*, Clemens wrote for local readers on such events as mine developments, earthquakes, court trials, Indian activities, and elections. Nevertheless, as Gerber points out, Clemens became best known as a jester. "He had not been with the *Enterprise* much more than a month when he published a hoax entitled 'Petrified Man' that started his reputation for audacity. In it he announced the discovery near Humboldt City of a petrified man."

In 1865, Clemens next signed on with the *Sacramento Union*, covering in a series of amusing letters, under the fictitious character of Mr. Brown, the newly opened passenger service between San Francisco and Honolulu. These letters are daring, their ideas and attitudes are far from elegant, and at times their language was blatantly rude.

However, for all of his early successes with bold humor and literary pranks, Mark Twain's most lasting and poignant achievement was his treatment of childhood, using the rich materials of his own Mississippi boyhood.

His own childhood was woefully short, which perhaps explains his fascination with children. Clemens's father, an ambitious but unsuccessful lawyer and businessman, was a solemn and austere personality, far different from Sam's more affectionate mother, Jane Lampton Clemens. In 1847, his father, John Clemens, died, leaving the family's support to his young sons. Not surprisingly, Sam's early years are filled with schemes for getting rich, schemes that were never to materialize despite all his dreams. Twain's circumstances, however, would change as he became a popular journalist and writer.

On February 2, 1870, he married Olivia Langdon of Elmira, New York, the daughter of Jervis Langdon, a member of upper New York genteel society who had made his fortune in coal and lumber. Olivia possessed the poise and grace that Twain longed for in a wife. However, emotionally, his marriage was not a total success. He did not realize that Olivia's cool exterior masked a fiery temperament inside. Furthermore, Mr. and Mrs. Langdon were skeptical about the humorist who courted their daughter, and their approval of the marriage was reluctant.

Later on, in the 1890s, a series of tragic events left their mark on the declining Mark Twain. His youngest daughter, Jean, was diagnosed as an epileptic, and his eldest daughter, Susy, died of meningitis while he and his wife were in Europe. Bad financial speculations left him bankrupt in the panic of 1893, while his physical and emotional health declined as well. His literary production of these years was mediocre in comparison to his past achievements. And yet in these last years, Twain was a much revered public figure, and the press sought him out for his opinions on a wide range of topics.

Mark Twain died in 1910, but his literary works ensured his immortality. His writing was both brilliant and charming, and yet it always demanded a heightened social consciousness and responsibility—from both his readers and himself.

The Story Behind the Story

In late November 1868, Samuel Clemens began to focus seriously on his relationship to Olivia Langdon, the twenty-two year old daughter of Jervis Langdon, a very successful businessman who made his fortune primarily from the coal business. As a result of severe back pain, Olivia was a former cripple, though much improved before she met Samuel Clemens. The Langdons were a very proper and prominent family, and Clemens had to work hard to win their approval of him. Indeed, Jervis Langdon subjected Clemens to a rigorous investigation, demanding the names of six individuals who would vouch for his character. Though Clemens supplied the requisite six names, Jervis called upon a former employee in San Francisco to interview the six references, and went even further in contacting some others who had not been designated. As a result of one of these investigations, a Presbyterian deacon responded to the inquiry by stating: "'I would rather bury a daughter of mine than have her marry such a fellow.'" (Emerson, *Mark Twain: A Literary Life*). For his part, Clemens expended considerable effort in convincing Olivia that he was a devout Christian. The couple eventually married her on February 2, 1870 in Elmira, New York and moved into a spacious home, complete with servants, in Buffalo. For a time, Olivia and Samuel would read the Bible together, but this did not last for long since he attached no credence to the Bible saving his soul and because he believed it to be filled with mythology. The writing of *Huckleberry Finn* served as a type of liberation from the civilizing and conforming to social convention which he had to endure in entering polite eastern society even before his marriage to Olivia. Through the character of his beloved Huck, Clemens could indulge his old values of independence, self-indulgence, laziness, skepticism, irreverence and forthrightness. Indeed, through the writing of *Huckleberry Finn*, Mark Twain had sought to recapture his childhood experiences in Hannibal, Missouri, the sleepy river town of Samuel Clemens' boyhood which would become the imaginative scene of archetypal innocence and idyllic childhood, the quintessential small town America, with its all its charm and potential and its social and political injustices. Though Twain left Hannibal as a teenager and he would return seven times as an adult to the place which held cherished childhood memories. Indeed, Hannibal became the fictionalized town of St. Petersburg in both *Tom Sawyer* and *Huckleberry Finn*.

Fiction as Survival

The similarity between the characters of Huckleberry Finn and Holden Caulfield (*The Catcher in the Rye*) have been the subject of critical debate. Both are adolescent boys trying to escape the danger and hypocrisy of the world they have inherited, and both are in pursuit of a better life. Huck is an impoverished and uneducated orphan who must raise himself in a corrupt and bigoted world where slavery is the law. Holden, the son of upper middle class parents, is a student in an expensive preparatory school, who *loves* his literature classes, the only subject which he is not failing. But despite their vastly different social and economic backgrounds, both Huck Finn and Holden Caulfield have been traumatized, albeit in different ways, and both must cope with their individual crises through the vehicle of fiction. And, as each one is the sole narrator of his story, they are in full control of the recounting of their individual histories.

The reality of *The Adventures of Huckleberry Finn* is that Huck must constantly construct a variety of fictions to keep Jim and himself alive, oftentimes involving a multiple layering of one fiction upon another—the compounding of a lie. Two examples from a multitude of instances will illustrate this point. Once such instance is the smallpox lie, which Huck invents when he encounters two white strangers on the river. The two men, suspicious that the raft may harbor a fugitive slave, are lead astray by Huck's tall tale that his pap is in a bad way, convincing these evildoers to help him out. And, when Huck succeeds in persuading these rascals to cooperate, their assistance requires further duplicity as they must not let others know that the threat of contagious disease is lurking in the background while looking out for their own well-being at the same time. "'Now, we're trying to do you a kindness; so you just put twenty miles between us, that's a good boy.'" Another such instance is the hilarious episode in Chapter 10 where Huck dresses up as a girl so he can go to town and find out the latest gossip about his and Jim's disappearance. Huck dons a dress and a bonnet that was taken from a floating house on the previous evening. "I put on the sun-bonnet and tied under my chin, and then for a body to look in and see my face was like looking down a joint of stove-pipe." Once Huck is inside the stranger's house, the web of lies grows more intricate with each of Huck's successive explanations. Huck presents himself as a girl on her way to an uncle on the other end of town. When the woman starts relating the local news, Huck learns that Pap has disappeared and that Jim is a prime suspect in Huck's supposed murder and, even worse, there is a reward for Jim's capture. He offers a variety of feminine names, but cannot keep them straight in his own mind. Shortly thereafter, he starts toying with the woman's sewing equipment, which results in the revelation that her young guest is really a boy who does not know how to thread a needle. Huck's response to this revelation is to further compound his lie by admitting the woman is right, while fabricating a tragic story about the terrible events that led him to try this disguise. Not only does the woman believe him, she has a great deal of sympathy for his plight and unwittingly saves his life and Jim's by revealing that her husband is on the lookout for the runaway slave. Though the potential for danger and violence is just beneath the surface of each episode, tragedy is forever mitigated by, and coexistent with a humorous spin in each instance.

Holden Caulfield is a teenage boy who is also rebelling against the hypocrisy of the world around him, refusing to conform to its expectations, and forever fantasizing about a highly romanticized utopian venue in which he can find solace and happiness For Holden Caulfield, it is his educated ability to call upon the great literary works, more specifically, the high ideals of the Arthurian legends, to provide the analogues necessary for surviving a world of hypocrisy and selfishness. The ethical principles of loyalty and good fellowship practiced by the Knights of the Roundtable, as well as the respect and dutiful service to women required by the courtly love tradition provide a place to which Holden can escape. Though these high ideals exist only as a literary convention, they nevertheless provide Holden with the only possible vehicle for self-expression and to the end provide a type of therapy. *The Catcher in the Rye*, in which he is the exclusive narrator, charts a series of episodes that take place during the course of approximately two days and is the story of the events leading up to his emotional breakdown and hospitalization in some unspecified mental health facility. There is no reason to believe that Holden will improve by talking to a mental health professional who is yet another representative of the adult world he seeks to escape. Nevertheless, for Holden, literature has provided him with a set of values to which he can aspire—the world of legend and high ideals as a response to the morally bankrupt world he is forced to live in. And, in a story of adolescent crisis, some of the dangers which Holden must confront are somewhat mitigated by J.D. Salinger's sense of humor—a playfulness with literary conventions and mythological associations. One can only hope that Holden will resort to the world of legend and high ideals as a response to the morally bankrupt world he is forced to live in.

Perhaps the overwhelming reality for both Huck Finn and Holden Caulfield is that life and fiction engage in an eternal exchange. Huck's rendition of his experiences is deliberately framed as an adventure story and it is his endless resourcefulness and unwavering talent for inventing elaborate explanations which literally saves both Jim and him from a terrible fate. Huck is the quintessential young boy who uses his imagination to save others. And, in so doing, Huck becomes a living legend—a hero who strives to make the world a better place to live, most especially in the potential loving relationship he forms with a runaway slave. Having accomplished this, the story ends with Huck, conscious of creating his own fictitious identity, vowing to avoid civilization. "And so there ain't nothing more to write about, and I am rotten glad of it, because if I'd 'a' knowed what a trouble it was to make a book I wouldn't 'a' tackled it.... But I reckon I got to light out for the territory ... because Aunt Sally she's going to adopt me and sivilize me, and I can't stand it."

List of Characters

Huckleberry Finn is the thirteen- or fourteen-year-old son of the town drunkard, Pap Finn, and the friend of Tom Sawyer. Like Jim, the escaped slave, Huck is superstitious, believing in such things as witches and the sinister omen of spiders crawling on his shoulder. "I got up and turned around in my tracks three times and crossed my breast every time; and then I tied up a little lock of my hair with a thread to keep the witches away." Eventually, Huck shows himself to be a true hero when he helps Jim escape his enslavement at the Phelps farm, a rescue mission made possible through Huck's and Tom's disguising of themselves. But, despite his rebellious nature and the fact that the adult world is unreliable at best, Huck nevertheless demonstrates a maturity and responsibility beyond his years, and made all the more poignant in that he never learned right from wrong, but instead acts according to what instinctively feels is the right way.

Pap Finn is the corrupt and drunken, fifty-year-old father of Huck. He is uneducated, immoral and prone to violence. He is audacious and will go to any absurd length to get what he wants, although he is totally unaware of his outrageous character. When he is murdered, Jim finds the body floating down the river, but decides to wait a long time before giving Huck the news.

Tom Sawyer is Huckleberry Finn's best friend and idol. We first make his acquaintance in the beginning of the novel when Tom organizes a group of robbers known as "Tom Sawyer's Gang." Indeed, the young Tom demonstrates leadership skills and a familiarity with adventure stories in his complex organization of the gang, which requires a pledge from each member to "write his name in blood." After this episode Tom drops out of the story until he reappears at Phelps farm and participates in the rescue of Jim.

Jim is Ms. Watson's Negro slave. He is very gullible and calls upon a variety of superstitions and folkloric remedies when in a difficult bind. In the beginning of the narrative, Tom and Huck, while hiding, trick Jim into thinking that witches have flown his body around the state and have hung his hat on a limb as proof that they were there. Jim's response is to consult his "hair-ball oracle" which was "as big as your fist, which had been took out of the fourth stomach of an ox, and he used to do magic with it." Later on in the story, when Jim learns that his owner plans to sell him down the river, he escapes with Huck, hoping to eventually make it up the Ohio River and thereby gain his freedom. When Jim is sold to Silas Phelps, Huck is instrumental in rescuing him. Always endearing, Jim not only depends on Huck and Tom for protection, but also displays parental feelings for the two boys. He "called us honey, and all the pet names he could think of." Ironically, Jim had already been freed much earlier by Miss Watson on her deathbed, although he only learns of this later on.

Widow Douglas is the well-intentioned widow of Judge Douglas who "adopts" Tom and tries to be a stabilizing influence in his life.

Judge Thatcher is the distinguished judge who safeguards Huck's $6,000 dollars so that Pap cannot lay claim to it. Later on, Huck and Tom each ask for $800 from their accounts in order to buy Jim from the Duke and the King.

Duke is a thirty-four-year-old printer who claims to be the heir of his great-great-grandfather, the Duke of Bridgewater and Jim and Huck indulge his game by calling him "Your Grace." Indeed, the Duke further claims to be both Dr. Armand de Montalban, the phrenologist, and the Shakespearean actor, David Garrick.

King is a seventy-year-old temperance lecturer, fortune teller and fraudulent preacher. Like his younger cohort, the Duke, the King makes many pompous statements about his various royal identities, which include the missing Dauphin of France, Louis the Seventeenth, and the son of Louis the Sixteenth. The King also pretends to be another famous Shakespearean actor, Edmund Kean the Elder. Once again, Jim and Huck indulge these pretensions by calling him "Your Majesty."

Summary and Analysis

Published in 1884, *The Adventures of Huckleberry Finn* continues the story of Tom Sawyer and Huckleberry Finn where *The Adventures of Tom Sawyer* leaves off. Indeed, Huck Finn implies that the difficulty for the reader to distinguish truth from fiction may possibly be continued in the sequel as *The Adventures of Tom Sawyer* "was made by Mr. Mark Twain, and he told the truth, mainly. There was things which he stretched, but mainly he told the truth."

Thus, *Huckleberry Finn* begins with Huck distancing himself from any responsibility for the tall-tales and other tamperings with the truth that may occur in this sequel to *Tom Sawyer*. Following this inaugural disclaimer, the story begins with Huck Finn reminding us that the two young heroes at St. Petersburg by the Mississippi are now rich, having previously found $6,000 dollars each from McDougal's cave. However, Judge Thatcher has invested the money and Huck is left to the care of the kindly Widow Douglas, and her sister, Miss Watson, "a tolerable slim old maid, with goggles," who lives with them. But Huck prefers to wear old rags. Having been first raised by his feckless father, Pap Finn, Huck has grown accustomed to a life of dodging the authorities and avoiding school at all costs. Indeed, a little further on in the story, when the very hostile and drunk Pap Finn returns to take possession of both the $6,000 and custody of his son, we find out how threatened Pap is by the idea of Huck learning to read and write. "You're educated, too, they say—can read and write. You think you're better'n your father, now, don't you, because he can't! *I'll* take it out of you." Needless to say, this dissolute upbringing has created the initial problem which Huck presents us with, namely his resistance to the Widow Douglas wanting to civilize him, an idea to which Huck's entire being is absolutely opposed. "The Widow Douglas she took me for her son, and allowed she would sivilize me; but it was rough living in the house all the time." Huck simply cannot understand, let alone abide, the Widow Douglas's style of domesticity and notions of proper behavior. "Pretty soon I wanted to smoke, and asked the widow to let me. But she wouldn't. She said it was a mean practice and wasn't clean.... That is just the way with some people." And, to further heighten the injustice, Huck also includes a brief but important detail about adult hypocrisy. "And she took snuff, too; of course that was all right, because she done it herself." Thus, Huck immediately presents us with unappealing portrait of his life with the Widow Douglas, and this description becomes the "landscape" against which he will forever rebel—a background of adults who, while seeking to impose strict regulations on adolescent behavior are nevertheless ineffectual, hypocritical and in the case of Huck's father, wholly irresponsible and dissolute in their own right.

The first of numerous rebellions against the civility of home and responsibility occurs just after Huck sets forth his observations as Tom starts "me-yeowing" under Huck's bedroom window, enticing his friend to scramble out the window to join him (**chapter 1**). At first, they attempt to play a trick on the lovable and gullible Jim, Miss Watson's slave, by slipping Jim's hat off his head and hanging it on a tree and then convincing him that witches were making noises (**chapter 2**). "Afterwards, Jim said the witches bewitched him and put him in a trance, and rode him all over the State." After a brief discussion of how Jim became conceited after regaling the other slaves with his bravado for confronting the devil, Tom and Huck meet with some other "adventurous" companions, including Joe Harper and Ben Rogers. The boys make a pledge to form a band of robbers called "Tom Sawyer's Gang," a pledge which requires each member to "write his name in blood." This is followed by a long list of restrictions and proscriptions and is thus a miming of the very same "civilizing" code of behavior against which Huck and Tom are determined to evade. "It swore every boy to stick to the band.... And nobody that didn't belong to the band could use that mark, and if he did he must be sued; and if he done it again he must be killed." Thus, Huck and Tom are invoking the very same societal means of rendering justice to those who violate its laws found in the "civilized" and hypocritical world of decency and self-righteousness. It is one of the numerous frightening scenes, replete with danger, violence and criminal behavior which is, at the same time, mitigated by the fact that it is merely an expression of childish fantasy and Twain's humor and social satire. The gang of robbers soon disbands after little Tommy Barnes, who has fallen asleep, is awakened scared and crying for his mother. When the gang makes fun of Tommy, he threatens to reveal their conspiracy and earns five cents hush money from Tom Sawyer, "who said we would all go home and meet next week and rob somebody and kill some people." This scene becomes one of the many instances in which Mark Twain's searing social commentary is conveyed through the vehicle of his young protagonists, Tom and Huck for despite their imaginative undertakings, the real world of social injustice and adult fecklessness is forever impinging on their happiness.

The following morning, Huck receives a sermon from the Widow Douglas when she sees his grimy clothes (**chapter 3**). The Widow has a good heart, and instead of scolding Tom, she encourages him to pray, but to little avail, for Huck has not seen any concrete proof of its effectiveness. "I says to myself, if a body can get anything they pray for, why don't Deacon Winn get back the money he lost on pork?" What is so poignant at this early stage in the narrative is that Huck has a low opinion of himself, believing that everyone he comes in contact with is better than him. "I thought it all out, and reckoned I would belong to the widow's [Providence], ... though I couldn't make out how he was going to be any better off then than what he was before, seeing I was so ignorant and so kind of low-down and ornery." Huck's feelings of inferiority extend as far as Tom Sawyer, whom he perceives as superior because Tom reads books and attends school. We also now learn a little bit about Pap Finn's legendary history as he relates that a body was found floating in the river, which some people believed to be Pap, though Huck considers him to be alive and dangerous.

Chapter 4 begins with Huck revealing that though he is not overjoyed with school, or with living in a house, he does not hate it the way he used to. Huck is also equally as vulnerable to superstition as Jim, as seen by his behavior when he knocks over the salt shaker at the breakfast table. "I reached for some of it as quick as I could, to throw over my should and keep off the bad luck." Unfortunately, lending credence to this myth is the coincident fact that Huck then goes outside only to find bootprints in the snow, an unmistakable sign that his father has been around. Recognizing that his father has designs on his money, Huck instinctively runs to Judge Thatcher and begs him to act as trustee of the six thousand dollars. Though the judge does not understand Huck's motives, he buys the account from Huck for one dollar. Huck's motive is to tell the truth to his father, mainly that he has no money. After leaving the judge, Huck decides to visit Jim, who possesses a hair-ball, supposedly coming from the stomach of an ox, which can predict the future. Huck wants to divine Pap's plans, but Jim ends up predicting so many things that he actually predicts nothing.

And, indeed, the unrelenting fact that adults forever disrupt childhood happiness and well-being is manifested when Huck comes home to find his alcoholic father waiting for him (**chapter 5**). Though Pap Finn is seldom around, whenever he makes an appearance, he creates trouble for his son. "'I've been in town two days, and I hain't hearing nothing but about you bein' rich.... That's why I come. You git me that money to-morrow—I want it.'" Not only has he abandoned his own child, he has no scruples about taking everything Huck owns. Moreover, he is more than willing to threaten violence when he perceives that his son may achieve a better life. "I'll lay for you, my smarty; and if I catch you about that school I'll tan you good." Nevertheless, Huck is not as afraid of Pap as he has been imagining.

Shortly thereafter, frustrated by Huck's unwillingness to yield to his demands for the money, Pap Finn decides to make his demand directly before Judge Thatcher. "[H]e went to Judge Thatcher's and bullyragged him, and tried to make him give up the money; but he couldn't, and then he swore he'd make the law force him." In so doing, Pap demonstrates a complete misapprehension of the judicial system and who it is supposed to protect. Furthermore, Pap's outrageous sense of entitlement produces a custody battle over his son, with the judicial system quickly shown to be an abysmal failure, indeed suffering from a genuine blindness, in its responsibility to protect children. "The judge and the widow went to law to get the court to take me away from him ... but it was a new judge ... so he said courts mustn't interfere and separate families if they could help it." Instead, the new judge naively states that he will reform the incorrigible Pap Finn, and so he "'dressed him up clean and nice ... and was just old pie to him, so to speak,'" but in the end Pap leaves the comfort of a his beautiful guest room, preferring to slide down a stanchion in order to get a "drunk as a fiddler" and, thus, forcing the new judge to admit the hopelessness of effecting a reform. When Pap later on has the temerity to seek Judge Thatcher a second time, the judicial proceedings are slow-moving and tedious, "appeared like they warn't ever going to get started on it," and in fact those proceedings deplete Huck of the little money he has, borrowing "two or three dollars off of the judge for [Pap], to keep from getting a cowhiding."

Once Pap regains control of himself, he hires a lawyer to sue Judge Thatcher for the money that once belonged to Huck (**chapter 6**). Although he occasionally catches Huck and beats him for going to school, Huck continues to go, to spite his father. Finally, in desperation, Pap kidnaps Huck and locks him in a cabin on a desolate spot along the Illinois shore, never letting Huck out of his sight for a moment. Here, a curious thing happens which accords with Twain's consummate skill in embedding a serious theme within a humorous story—namely, Huck thoroughly enjoying his truancy, "laying off comfortable all day, smoking and fishing, and no books nor study," and reveling in his freedom to resume cussing "because Pap had no objections." Indeed, Pap encourages his son to swear. And, although he complains about not getting justice from his government, when he has had all the anxiety and expense of raising a son, we know this to be a sham. One the contrary, he is neither a good citizen nor a good father. Furthermore, Pap's harangue allows Twain to make one of his many sharp indictments of racial bigotry. Pap looks like a complete and ignorant fool when he berates the government for allowing a black college professor to vote along with a white man like himself. The chapter concludes with Huck wishing for an opportunity to break away from Pap.

While out catching some fish for breakfast, Huck discovers an opportunity to facilitate his eventual getaway from Pap (**chapter 7**). He spots an abandoned canoe drifting by, wades out to grab it and then hides the canoe in the woods. When Pap heads out to town to sell some logs, Huck seizes the opportunity to execute his elaborate escape plan, a plan designed to make everyone think Huck was murdered. This is essential since Huck is running away from all the authority figures in his life and the report of his decease will buy him time. Huck embarks on his journey and stops on nearby Jackson's Island as his temporary hideout, where he falls asleep in the canoe. When he wakes up, he hears his father rowing toward his island. Huck unhitches the canoe and floats downstream as quietly as possible. Huck wakes up after daybreak, "feeling rested and ruther comfortable and satisfied" (**chapter 8**) as he lies in the grass enjoying the sun, the trees and some friendly-looking squirrels. But his peaceful coexistence with nature is disrupted by the sound of cannon fire. When Huck identifies the source as a ferry boat, he understands that it contains a search party looking for his dead body. Indeed, the ferry comes dangerously close to the island, affording Huck the ability to see the familiar faces of Pap, Tom Sawyer, the Widow Douglas, and Judge Thatcher, as well as others. However, the brush with danger notwithstanding, Huck is overcome by loneliness after the ferry passes and resolves to go to sleep, declaring that "[t]here ain't no better way to put in time when you are lonesome." However, after three days on the island, Huck's loneliness is replaced by feelings of terror when he stumbles upon the remains of a campfire, signaling that he is not alone. To his great joy and relief, Huck discovers that the stranger is Jim, who is likewise on the run from Miss Watson. At first, Huck is shocked because in his world a runaway slave is a criminal. Nevertheless, Huck immediately acknowledges his obligation to Jim. He promised never to divulge Jim's secret and he intends to honor that commitment. This becomes a pivotal moment in Huck's character as he must resolve a conflict between legal and ethical demands and remain true to his word and feelings. In so doing, Huck makes a complete break with "home" and all the social injustices that surround it.

Huck and Jim are now two fellow outcasts embarking on their new life (**chapter 9**) and soon find a cavern to set up temporary housekeeping. It begins to rain for several days almost immediately upon their arrival and after a few more days the river floods. Shortly thereafter, they find a raft and on another outing, they climb into the window of a two-story house that's floating by, where the find the body of a murdered man. Jim assumes the role of a loving parent when he covers the man's face to keep Huck from seeing it. After they ransack the provisions, they return to the security of their island. The next morning Huck wonders aloud how the dead man was killed (**chapter 10**), with Jim pronouncing it bad luck to even discuss it, adding that unburied corpses are more likely to haunt people than buried ones. The chapter closes with the beginning of a hilarious episode of Huck dressing up as a girl so he can go to town and find out the latest news about him and Jim. He puts on a dress and a bonnet that they took from the floating house the night before. After making his way to the mainland, Huck finds himself outside the house of someone who has just moved into town. **Chapter 11** demonstrates Huck's resourcefulness in telling a lie, although he ultimately makes some critical mistakes. Huck enters the woman's house and presents himself as a girl on her way to an uncle on the other end of town. When the woman starts relating the local news, Huck learns that Pap has disappeared and that Jim is a prime suspect in Huck's supposed murder. In fact, the woman's husband is planning to hunt for Jim and collect the reward. Shortly thereafter, Huck's nervousness causes him to lose his cover. When he starts toying with the woman's sewing equipment and reveals that he cannot thread a needle, she recognizes that he is in fact a boy. Huck's response is to further compound his lie by admitting the woman is right, while fabricating a tragic story about the terrible events that led him to try this disguise. Not only does the woman believe him, she has a great deal of sympathy for his plight, offering him advice on how to maintain his feminine cover. When Huck returns to Jim, the two friends set out on their long journey down the Mississippi River.

Chapters 12 and **13** deal with Huck and Jim's first adventure while on the Mississippi. Huck begins by recounting that Jim has built a wigwam on the raft to protect their belongings and describes the sights they see, including the city of St. Louis, and their daily routine of going ashore each night to buy food and to "borrow" things they cannot afford. Shortly thereafter, they come upon a disabled steamboat, named the Walter Scott. After climbing aboard the steamboat, Huck and Jim hear the voices of three thieves, and learn of their murderous intention. When Huck decides to get out, Jim informs him that raft has broken loose. Huck then decides to find the usual skiff that is used for transporting people in shallow water and they silently slip away (**chapter 13**). Once they are free, Huck expresses concern for the thieves they have left stranded, "how dreadful it was, even for murderers, to be in such a fix," and he tells Jim he wants to help them. In order to save the three criminals from almost certain drowning, Huck tells a ferryboat captain an elaborate tale about his family being stranded on the disabled steamboat and feels better for having assisted the three undesirables. "I wished the widow knowed about it.... I judged she would be proud of me for helping these rapscallions, because rapscallions and dead-beats is the kind the widow and good people takes the most interest in." It appears that Huck is interested in saving lost souls. In **chapter 14**, Huck and Jim discuss the Old Testament story of the wise King Solomon, who was asked to settle a dispute over who was the real mother of the baby that one of them was carrying. While Jim insists that no really wise man would have suggested cutting a baby in two as a solution to a dispute, Huck maintains that he is missing the point. In the end, Huck gives in to Jim, demonstrating a willingness to give in to a slave and, further, that Jim has the temerity to argue with a white person. A radical shift in self-perception has taken place on the part of both Huck and Jim.

By Huck's reckoning, they are only three nights away from Cairo, Illinois, signaling a free state and the end of Jim's status flight from danger (**chapter 15**). However, they run into a heavy fog, signaling their entry into a dangerous situation, and Huck temporarily loses both the raft and Jim while attempting to find a place to dock it. What follows is a terrifying description of the river. "If you think it ain't dismal and lonesome out in a fog that way, by yourself, in the night, you try it once—you'll see." When Huck finally locates the raft, Jim is sound asleep at the steering oar, and there is a shift in tone from serious to mischievous as Huck transforms the fear and anxiety that both have experienced into a prank. After awakening Jim and pretending as if they never had been separated by the fog, Jim assumes he must have dreamed the whole thing, and he goes through an elaborate interpretation of what each detail symbolized. But when he's finished, Huck shows him that it really did happen, and that Jim is in fact just been the butt of a joke. Jim feels betrayed by Huck, stating that he felt like dying when he thought he had lost his friend. Nevertheless, the two continue their journey and as they get closer to Cairo, they both become anxious, though for much different reasons. Jim's nervousness is the result of getting closer to the long-awaited freedom he deserves, while Huck's apprehension is more complex for, although he senses it is right to help Jim escape his terrible lot, and that he has made a promise to a friend, he is, at the same time, breaking the laws of the same society he is running from (**chapter 16**). At first, prompted by Jim's stated plan to enlist the help of an Abolitionist to "steal" back the children that were so wrongfully taken from him, Huck becomes frightened and starts to paddle back. But this changes when Jim acknowledges Huck as the only white man who ever kept his promise to him. A defining moment occurs when Huck encounters two men who looking for runaway slaves. Faced with the choice of doing the ethical thing or succumbing to an unjust law that requires turning in his friend Jim, Huck decides to protect Jim and tells the men he's traveling with a white man. Curiously, though, Huck still doesn't understanding that he did the right thing— he acts according to instinct and what feels right in the moment. "I warn't man enough," he tells us. "Hadn't the spunk of a rabbit." By the end of this chapter, the raft is split in two by a carelessly piloted steamboat. Separated from Jim, Huck makes his way to shore only to find himself surrounded by a pack of barking dogs.

Chapters 17 and **18** contain an elaborate satirical commentary on the society in which both Huck and his author spent their childhoods. As the barking dogs are directed to quiet down by a command from within the house, Huck receives suspicious directions to make his way slowly to the Grangerford house. Once inside, Huck finds himself surrounded by men aiming pistols at him. Once they become satisfied that Huck is not a Shepherdson, their behavior changes radically as the men express concern for his welfare and accept his story about being an orphan who fell overboard from a steamboat. Huck is invited to move in with Buck, a family member about his own age. For his part, Huck forgets the hostile introduction and instead focuses on what he sees as the marks of a fine, educated, aristocratic Southern family. While the naïve Huck recounts how everything appears on the surface, Twain wants us to look beyond appearances to see the true hypocrisy of the house, such as the interior decorations, which include the "outlandish [chalk] parrot" on each side of the clock, and a "cat made of crockery," a décor truly in bad taste when held up to scrutiny. Another important detail is related by Huck when he talks about the drawings left behind by the now deceased, young Emmeline Grangerford. From Huck's perspective, the pictures are dark and gloomy, one in particular—an incomplete drawing of a young woman which is mainly concealed behind a curtain except during the absurd celebration of Emmeline's birthday when the family hangs flowers on it. Huck manages to make one inciteful comment, though he says it seriously. "I reckoned that with her disposition she was having a better time in the graveyard."

The satire continues in **chapter 18**. It begins with Huck's straightforward appraisal of the colonel. "Col. Grangerford was a gentleman, you see. He was a gentleman all over; and so was his family." And his family follows rigid rules of propriety, including a dress code. But right after this description, Huck makes an alarming observation. "Each person had their own nigger to wait on them," adding that the slave assigned to him had an easy time, because Huck wasn't used to being waited on. Shortly thereafter, Huck relates how wonderful the Grangerfords are as he recounts a conversation in which he asks Buck about the family feud with the Shepherdsons. From this conversation, Huck learns several pieces of information, namely that it is not clear exactly when the feud started; there may be no one left who remembers what the original argument was about; that a large number of people from both families have been killed in the feud and that many others have been injured. Finally, there is the extraordinarily misplaced and inappropriate admiration which Buck has for the Shepherdsons and the murderous feud they are embroiled in. By the end of this chapter, Huck finally becomes so disgusted that he can no longer relate the details lest he become sick himself. However, it is also important to recognize that Huck is still slow to learn the real lesson that surface appearances are exactly that and require further scrutiny. Huck also tells us in this chapter how he gets back together with Jim, who has by now repaired the damaged raft. Huck is very happy to escape the Grangerfords as he and Jim agree that "there warn't no home like a raft, after all."

In **chapters 19 and 20** we meet the duke and the king, characters who will be with Huck longer than any other characters in the book, including Jim, who almost disappears from the story until chapter 30, an absence which is highly curious and the subject of critical debate as to whether or not it weakens the narrative in any way. **Chapter 19** begins with one of the longest descriptions in the book of the beauty of being on the river. "[T]hen the nice breeze springs up, and comes fanning you from over there, so cool and fresh, and sweet to smell, on account of the woods and flowers." Huck meets the duke and king while paddling a canoe near the shore to look for berries. One of them looks to be about 70 years old, with "an old battered-up slouch hat on, and a greasy blue woolen shirt," while the other is judged to be about 30, "dressed about as ornery." In reality, they are two con men in a great hurry to get away from somebody, and Huck agrees to let them come back to the raft with him. **Chapter 20** shows the two con artists in action as they visit a small town and steal a few dollars. In one of the most hilarious episodes in the novel, they plan a show consisting of the most memorably scenes from three Shakespearean plays: the balcony scene from *Romeo and Juliet*, in which the old man (the king) will play Juliet; Hamlet's soliloquy from *Hamlet* (chapter 21); and the sword fight from *Richard III*. The performances are a complete fraud designed to bilk money from the naïve country "jakes" as the duke assures him. By the end of the chapter, Huck is fed up with kings.

In **chapters 21 to 23**, Huck describes his visit to a small town in Arkansas in the company of the duke and the king. **Chapter 21** begins with the two con men getting ready for the Shakespearean performance they intend to give in the towns they visit along the river. Needless to say, true to the fraudulent character of the duke, he does not know nearly as much about Shakespeare as he pretends, though he can easily dupe the others on the raft. As to Hamlet's "to be or not to be" soliloquy, the duke presents it as a hodgepodge of lines from *Macbeth*, *Romeo and Juliet*, as well as other plays. The speech is hilarious and shows Mark Twain to be a consummate writer of parodies. As fraudulent as it is, Huck is impressed. "It seemed like he was just born for it; and when he had his hand in and was excited, it was perfectly lovely the way he would rip and tear and rair up behind when he was getting it off." Indeed, in the circular that the duke prints to advertise their show, he bills himself as David Garrick and the king as Edmund Kean, two famous 19th century actors of the Romantic period. And the circular has Shakespeare's name misspelled. Huck also gives us a careful description of the dilapidated town and its illiterate residents. The men are lethargic do-nothings, and their energies are focused mainly on obtaining chewing tobacco. This landscape stands in stark contrast to the deceptive gentility of the

Grangerford household. Along with many townspeople, Huck witnesses the cold-blooded shooting of a tough-talking drunk who insults a well-dressed man named Colonel Sherburn. When the drunk ignores Sherburn's warning, the colonel kills him. Instead of showing concern for this murderous deed, the crowd immediately sets to arguing over who will get the "front-row seats" to see him take his last breath. "Well by and by somebody said Sherburn ought to be lynched. In about a minute everybody was saying it; so away they went, mad and yelling, and snatching down every clothes-line they come to, to do the hanging with." Then, ironically, though no one tried to prevent the murder, the mob decides to lynch Colonel Sherburn.

When the mob disbands in **chapter 22**, Huck sneaks into a circus and is easily fooled by the pre-arranged act he watches. Even when he discovers that it has been planned, he still believes that the ringmaster was fooled. "Well all through the circus they done the most astonishing things; and all the time, that clown carried on so it most killed the people. The ring-master couldn't ever say a word to him but he was back at him quick as a wink with the funniest things a body ever said." **Chapter 23** is mostly comedy, beginning with Huck's description of how the king and the duke cheat the townspeople out of nearly $500 and get away unscathed. The way they make their living prompts Jim to ask Huck if he isn't surprised at "de way dem kings carries on," which then leads Huck into a long monologue on the terrible behavior of kings. Huck cites Henry VIII as a typical kingly rascal, "My, you ought to seen Henry the Eight when he was in blossom. He *was* a blossom. He used to marry a new wife every day, and chop off her head next morning" and then attributes to him everything he can think of from English history, similar to the previous conflation of plays in the duke's recitation of Hamlet's soliloquy. The next morning Huck awakes to find Jim pining for his family. It is a heartbreaking moment, with Huck observing that Jim cares for his family as much as white people care for theirs. "It don't seem natural," he adds, "but I reckon it's so." The chapter ends with Jim telling a harrowing story about a time he slapped his four-year-old daughter for not obeying him. When he found out that that she was suffering from scarlet fever, he was overcome with grief and begged God to forgive him, because he would never forgive himself.

Chapter 24 begins with the longest episode in the book, extending to **chapter 30**. As the duke and the king lay plans to defraud some townspeople out of their money, Jim complains that it is difficult to stay tied up in the cramped quarters of the wigwam while the others are away all day. Twain's solution, spoken by the duke, is to allow Jim to show himself on the raft during daylight because the planned swindle will keep Huck and the men in town for several days, Jim could not be held captive in the wigwam during all that time. At this time, Huck has some store-bought clothes the thieves were able to get with the money they took in from their outrageous Shakespearean performance, and he will billed as a servant. The plan is for them to hail a steamboat between towns, then arrive in the next town and claim they've traveled from St. Louis or Cincinnati. On the way, they offer a ride to a young man who is waiting for the boat himself, and the king initiates a conversation that turns out to be very profitable. It seems that a wealthy villager just died while expecting his brothers from England and that the brothers have not made an appearance. As the king "casually" conducts his inquiry, the young man reveals everything and then is dropped off at the steamboat. Huck, of course, recognizes the king's duplicitous agenda as he watches as the two imposters feign unbearable grief at having arrived too late to console their dying brother. Huck also observes how the simple people of the town erupt with sympathy for these two "mournful" travelers. "It was enough to make a body ashamed of the human race."

Chapter 25 opens with the king and the duke about to scam the family of the dead Peter Wilks. It is interesting to note that Huck reacts to the three Wilks' daughters more tenderly than he does to anyone else he meets in the book and, as a result, the scam causes him endless moral grief. But Huck continues with the charade because he must consider Jim's highly precarious status at the moment while correctly understanding that the two impostors would have no misgivings about betraying a runaway slave. Indeed, Huck is just as much a captive as Jim. And although the duke and king have now managed to obtain six thousand dollars in gold from the Wilks scam, the king becomes greedy for more, hoping to rob some girls as well. Huck finds the plan utterly disgusting in its successful execution. However, when the town doctor arrives on the scene, he recognizes the scam and laughs at the king, especially for his awful imitation of a British accent. The doctor denounces the thieves. Unbelievably, the daughters elect to have themselves defrauded as they are too caught up in the mob sentiment for the crooks. The chapter ends with the king throwing a sarcastic remark at the doctor. **Chapter 26** begins with Huck telling another of his great lies to the misguided sisters, posing as the men's "valley" and weaving another lie about living in England. However, the youngest sister, Joanna, is not duped and Huck is soon in over his head. To buy himself time to come up with another lie, Huck pretends to choke on a chicken bone. Huck soon decides to return the money to the misguided sisters. But, while he is in the midst of searching for the money, the men come upstairs and he is forced to hide behind a curtain. When he sees the king and duke hide the money inside a mattress and then leave the room, Huck takes the money to his room and waits until everyone is asleep.

In **Chapter 27**, Huck sneaks downstairs in the middle of the night in order to hide the money for safekeeping. When he hears someone coming, he immediately stashes the gold in the dead man's half-opened coffin, though he is afraid it will be discovered the next day by the undertaker. When the scene shifts to the undertaker and his style of caring for the bereaved we are again reminded of Twain's consummate skill as a humorist. Huck describes in some detail how the "softest, glidingest, stealthiest man I ever see" manages to conduct the funeral services while "making no more sound than a cat." Though Huck resolves to write to Mary Jane to tell her where to find the money, he is also afraid that it may result in her digging up nothing but the remains of her uncle. The day after the funeral finds the girls' "uncles" selling the household slaves to two traders, with the sons going to one and the mother to the other. The only mitigating fact for Huck is that he knows the sale is illegal and will be nullified in a few days. The chapter concludes with Huck succeeding in swindling the swindlers as he tells the king that the slaves stole the money and, further, because they have been sold, they cannot hope to recover it. **Chapter 28** opens with Huck consoling Mary Jane over the king's decision to sell the household slaves. Indeed, Huck is so concerned with reassuring her that he tells her the truth while explaining that the slaves will be back within two weeks. Huck even surprises himself and interrupts the narrative to wonder about it. Furthermore, since he's already taken the plunge, he continues to tell Mary Jane more of the truth, though he leaves out some details. Mary Jane consents to Huck's plan to expose the thieves, regain her money and get away safely himself. Once the details are worked out, Mary Jane promises to pray for Huck. Huck's reaction is quite interesting. In keeping with his low sense of self-esteem, he compares himself to Judas, the disciple who betrayed Christ and turned him over to the Roman soldiers. And, accordingly, he thinks that praying for him is a monumental task for a mere girl to take on. Nevertheless, Huck tells us how he feels about Mary Jane, and it sounds as though he may possibly love her. Unfortunately, just as the king and duke are selling off the last pieces of the family property, a crowd comes from the steamboat landing, loudly announcing the arrival of two other men who claim to be the brothers of the deceased Peter Wilks and, thus, the final recipient of the buried treasure is anybody's guess.

One would expect the arrival of the real Wilks brothers in **chapter 29** to signal an uncontested and appropriate allocation of the money. However, the world of *Huckleberry Finn* is fictional and far from rational, with Twain's trenchant satire providing the context for the events about to unfold. Here, we see the townspeople revealing themselves to be so gullible and blind to the most obvious evidence, that it is not possible for anyone to feel sympathy for them. Indeed, their lack of judgment leads to a ridiculous scenario in which they turn the "investigation'" of the two newcomers into a circus, cheering the conflicting claims of the two pairs of men, and egging them on to further outrageous statements. Even more astonishing is how brazenly and unflinchingly the king sticks to his imposture, despite all evidence to the contrary, including his forged signature of Peter Wilks. But sound judgment enters the scene when the town lawyer returns from a business trip and joins the doctor in backing the two new arrivals. At one point, these two men question Huck about England, and he finds he can't fool them as easily as he did Joanna in an earlier scene. But the lawyer lets him off gently, telling him he isn't much of a liar. When the townspeople call for the body to be dug up, the scene becomes ghoulish. Huck is dragged to the cemetery, along with the cheering mob, the two imposters, and the real brothers. When the coffin is raised and opened, however, the sight of the gold entrances everyone there, including the man who has been holding Huck by the wrist. Huck manages to escape the mob and reach his raft, much to the delight of Jim, who has been waiting several days without any word. As the raft begins to move, Huck realizes that he is once again free of the civilized society he fears so much. However, the joy is short-lived as he soon detects a familiar sound and understands that the king and the duke escaped right behind and are pursuing the raft. **Chapter 30** continues with the duke and king in pursuit of Huck. The king's first impulse is to accuse Huck of trickery, but Huck does some fast talking and the matter is quickly forgotten as their mutual distrust takes the heat off Huck. When the two men drink themselves to sleep, Huck tells Jim all that has transpired.

Chapter 31 begins lazily and unprofitably, which produces a problem for the two impostors. Once they have moved far enough to be free of any word-of-mouth gossip, the thieves try their hand at such things as temperance lectures, dance instruction, missionary work, mesmerizing, and doctoring, none of which schemes is successful. The king and duke become moody and secretive, and this becomes problematic for Huck and Jim, since they recognize that these two impostors have no scruples. Huck concludes that they must be planning to rob a house or a store, incapable of imagining that their conspiracy may be far more diabolical. They soon stop at "a shabby village named Pikesville." The king goes in first, and Huck and the duke follow several hours later. When they get to town, they find the king drunk, and the duke begins arguing with him. Huck does not waste a second in seizing an opportunity for him and Jim to escape. He takes off for the raft and never looks back. Jim, however, is gone, and Huck soon learns that the king has identified him as a runaway slave and sold his interest in the $200 reward for $40. Huck then considers writing to Miss Watson and telling her where Jim is, believing that Jim would be happier in familiar surroundings, but decides against this because he believes that Miss Watson, and everyone else who knows Jim, would never again treat him well. When he tries to pray, "the words wouldn't come," and he thinks he knows why. "It was because my heart warn't right; it was because I warn't square; it was because I was playing double." Huck wants God's forgiveness, though he doesn't really feel sorry for helping Jim and realizes that "you can't pray a lie." Thus, he decides to do the right thing first by writing to Miss Watson with the full story, and then praying later. But things are not so facile. Although the letter is a confession, a first for Huck, he tears it up. Jim, he decides, is a good person, who really cares for him; and the feeling is mutual.

Chapter 32 presents us with an entirely new situation for Huck as he arrives at the Phelps farm. For the first time in the novel, he is at a loss for words and does not know what to say. To Huck's great relief, the mistress of the house gives him a warm reception and introduces Huck to her children as their cousin Tom. She also tells him to call her Aunt Sally. When she questions him about her family, he tries to answer her questions but is saved from real embarrassment by the arrival of her husband. Sally tells Huck to hide under the bed so that she can play a trick on her husband for having missed meeting their guest. After a few minutes, she pulls out Huck from his hiding place and introduces him as Tom Sawyer. Huck is overjoyed to hear who he is and relieved because he will now be able to answer all of Sally's questions about the Sawyer family. "[I]t was like being born again, I was so glad to find out who I was.... I had told them more about my family than ever happened to any six Sawyer families. So heavily has he imbedded himself in deception that he decides he must find Tom before the rest of the family so that he can explain the predicament of pretending to be Tom Sawyer.

Chapter 33 begins with Huck's mission to find Tom Sawyer whom he meets in a wagon along the way. For his part, Tom, of course, is frightened by what he thinks is Huck's ghost, the result of several tiers of Hucks lying. "Lookyhere, warn't you ever murdered *at all?* But Huck soon convinces him that he is very much alive and persuades Tom to play along with the mistaken identity. When Huck tells Tom his plan to help Jim escape, Tom begins to respond and then stops. After thinking for a moment, he says he will help Huck steal Jim from his Uncle Silas. Ironically, Huck is astounded, and his opinion of Tom Sawyer is diminished for Tom, who is from a good family, is now agreeing to help Huck in this "dirty, low-down business." But irony can be easily explained. Though Huck does not yet know this, Tom knows that Jim is already a free man and his acquiescence in Huck's scheme is a mere charade. Now that Tom has agreed to help, he and Huck work out the first part of the plan—Tom's arrival at his uncle Silas' house. As Huck expects, Tom arrives with style, attracting the whole family outside to see who the stranger is. "He warn't a boy to meeky along up that yard like a sheep, no, he come ca'm and important, like a ram. After masquerading as a traveler from Ohio, he plays a trick on Aunt Sally and then announces that he is, in fact, Tom's brother Sid. This makes him even more welcome than he was before, and it also ensures that both boys will be able to stay for as long as they need to. Huck soon learns that the townspeople are aware of the two impostors, the king and the duke, and he and Tom sneak into town at night to warn them. When they get there, the men have been tarred and feathered and tied to a rail, about to be run out of town. Despite all the heartache the two thieves have caused Huck, he still feels sympathy for them. Huck's sensitivity once again manifests itself, and he becomes troubled by the fate these two scoundrels have met.

Chapter 34 finds all the preparations for Jim's escape ready to go. Tom suggests that he and Huck each devise a plan and then decide which is better. Once again, Huck's feelings of inferiority are revealed as he feels outclassed by Tom and that his friend's plan will be far superior to anything he can think of. Ironically, the plan that Huck presents is practical, straightforward and based on real experience of life on the river, a plan true to Huck's character. On the other hand, Tom wants Jim's escape to be an adventure, conducted in style. Huck's response, of course, is that it is by far the superior plan. "It was worth fifteen of mine for style, and would make Jim just as free a man as mine would, and maybe get us all killed besides." Yet, for all of Huck's acquiescence, he still feels guilty about involving the superior Tom Sawyer in the illegal act of freeing Jim. **Chapter 35** continues the elaborately-conceived scheme, "dark, deep-laid plans" for Jim's escape. And, once again, there is a sharp contrast between the characters of Huck and Tom evidenced by the two boys approach problems. Tom laments the fact that freeing Jim is simple to the point of embarrassment to any self-respecting adventurer. More specifically for Tom are the depressing details of the Phelps Farm: Uncle Silas is too trusting and the makeshift prison would be so flimsy that they would they would have to invent difficulties. But Huck has a problem with this. Though he is in awe of Tom's personal style, Huck's first priority is to get Jim out and run off with him, and he keeps asking Tom why they cannot choose the simple, expedient plan. But Tom has no patience for this nagging. "Why, hain't you ever read any books at all?" Tom insists on following the "best [literary] authorities" on the subject of escaping prisoners and all the work and equipment necessary for taking hostages—rope ladders, and moats, and digging out of a prison with a fork? Huck simply does not have Tom's literary mastery of genuine adventure stories and he feels diminished for his lack of Tom's "learning." Nevertheless, the boys go with Tom's complicated scheme. It is interesting to note that for all of Tom's bluster, he is the more conventional of the two, the one who insists on following rules, albeit here the rules of literary convention, while Huck remains the radical one, willing to break whatever rules or laws that might stand in the way of his doing the right thing. The chapter concludes with Tom directing Huck to steal some knives.

Chapters 36 and **37** continue with the hilarious particulars of putting their plan into effect, a plan gratuitously complicated and time-consuming. Much of the humor of these chapters stems from the ridiculous household items that Tom deems necessary to achieving the desired effect of danger and peril that he has read of in his adventure books. Mark Twain also finds a place to interject his own opinion about people who insist on rigidly obeying the law until they become ridiculous. After expending a great deal of time and effort digging with their small knives, Tom is compelled to admit that this method is destined to fail, despite what the books may say. Huck is very receptive to Tom's admission that this part of the plan will not work.

In chapters 38 and **39**, Tom continues to impose extraordinarily time-consuming measures in order to achieve the perilous effects which he insists on imposing on Jim's escape. To this end, Tom fills Jim's cabin with snakes, spiders, and rats. He gives him a plant that has to be watered with tears. While these details are hilarious in themselves, there is also a grim reality which cannot be ignored, namely, the cruel treatment to which Jim is subjected, made all the more grave in that Jim has known only a life of slavery and the anguish of having been torn apart from family members who are living under the same unjust system. Furthermore, Jim is highly superstitious, cannot read and certainly has no knowledge of adventure stories that Tom wants to bring to life—in a work Jim is vulnerable and gullible, and would probably think all this nonsense is a necessary part of his becoming free. Nevertheless, Huck remains susceptible to Tom's "superior learning" and plays along with his schemes. Indeed, it can be inferred that Twain himself is poking fun at Tom's character, such as the coat-of-arms scene in which Tom hides his incompetence from

Huck. There's a direct parallel between this scene and the one in which the duke faked his way through Hamlet's soliloquy. The strong implication is that Tom is somehow similar to that lowlife, who helped the king betray Huck and Jim for a few dollars. The culmination of these gratuitous details is the anonymous note Tom sends to his aunt and uncle, advising them to escape what is about to take place—because, according to the books he has read, these notes are an important component of an adventure.

The events surrounding Jim's elaborate escape unfold in **chapters 40** and **41**. Tom's anonymous note results in a gathering of neighboring farmers, all of whom are armed and poised to confront the thieves they think are coming to steal Silas Phelps' property. Huck is frightened by the prospect of these armed men trying interfering with the escape. Tom, however, is elated. Nevertheless, the escape takes place under two auspicious conditions—it is so dark, the farmers cannot see their intended target, and the dogs, which are part of the family, run right past the boys whom they recognize. Having evaded their attackers, they reach the canoe Huck has hidden and arrive at the island where he left the raft. It is only at this juncture that they discover that Tom has taken a bullet in the calf. This wound comports perfectly with Tom's love of special effects. As he bandages his wound, Tom gives orders for carrying out the rest of the escape plan, though Huck and Jim consult privately about how to handle the situation. Most poignantly, Jim declares that getting medical attention for Tom's injury is more important than him gaining his long-awaited freedom, especially in light of the gratuitous mistreatment that Tom has inflicted upon him. Huck finds a doctor for Tom, but the man won't share the tiny canoe with him and thus Huck ends up back at Aunt Sally's while the doctor goes to the island to treat Tom. Meanwhile, some o f the neighborhood women have seen the bizarre collection of items in the cabin and declare them the work of a crazy person.

Chapters 42 and **43** are the finale to Huck's narrative. Before Huck can get back to the raft, Tom and Jim have been captured by the doctor and with the assistance of a crowd, they are brought home. Jim's hands are tied, and Tom is carried on a mattress. Surprisingly, impressed by Jim's magnanimous solicitation for Tom, the doctor becomes Jim's advocate, expressing concern for Jim's welfare and well-being. Huck notes that while the farmers take the doctor's advice, they have not been motivated to remove Jim's chains. In a rapid acceleration of the plot, Tom confesses to Aunt Sally how he and Huck engineered the escape. And Tom's Aunt Polly arrives to tell Aunt Sally who her two guests really are. What follows is some very good news —Tom announces that Jim has been a free man for two months and Jim reveals that Huck's father is dead, which means that Huck's $6,000 is safe and waiting for him at home. The problem is that, for Huck, home is not where everyone else thinks it is. Having observed a lot of civilization from the vantage point of his raft, Huck declares that he will "light out for the territory," to those places which have not achieved statehood and or been encroached by civilization. "I been there before," he says, and it doesn't have much to offer him . I'd 'a' knowed what a trouble it was to make a book I wouldn't 'a' tackled it ... But I reckon I got to light out for the territory ... because Aunt Sally she's going to adopt me and sivilize me, and I can't stand it." Sadly, Eden does not exist, except as a flight of imagination.

Critical Views

DAVID E.E. SLOANE ON THE DEVELOPMENT OF A "RAFT ETHIC"

The chapters comprising Huck and Jim's initial raft voyage down the Mississippi are crucial to the shaping of Twain's positive vision and, along with important expansions of our understanding of the significance of the raft in chapter 19, they establish the philosophy that endows the power of the river with the undertow of humanity. Huck and Jim come to a higher level of relationship which is the basis for Huck's final powerful decision to go to hell. Even as Huck and Jim slide below the tip of Jackson's Island, Huck says that his tricky campfire "played it as low-down on them as I could," revealing his ambivalence about helping Jim. When Huck plays tricks on Jim and is reprimanded, he and Jim together create a better practical ethic than others provided them by American society, thus continuing the pattern of rejecting the ethics of the small town represented by Miss Watson and Pap. In the colorful description of the Mississippi flatboatmen, so long excised from the standard texts, Huck is shown further kindness as a "cub." The raft world allows for a finer ethic, formed in the natural background of "the big river," which Huck and Jim develop for themselves as they discuss pragmatism, kings, and right treatment versus trash-like treatment of friends.

Twain maintains excitement through descriptive details interwoven with philosophic discussions such as the one concerning "borrowing." Local details of the river foreshadow the raftsmen chapter, as even a "tow-head" is carefully described—with vernacular phrases—as "a sand-bar that has cotton-woods on it as thick as harrow-teeth." Huck rejects Jim's gossipy reasoning about their escape from Mrs. Loftus's husband by saying that he doesn't care what the reason was that they weren't caught just so long as they weren't—a mode of expressing his tension as aptly restrained as in Hemingway's heroes. Jim also mentions that they would have been returned to "the same old town" again. The opposite state of their present life is thus defined at the outset of the voyage. In comparison, the building of a comfortable raft, with floor elevated above steamboat waves and a shelter for protection from rain and sun, is detailed. Even the rules of navigation for safety from steamboats are outlined, foreshadowing a dramatic moment to follow.

Most important is the formation of a special raft ethic, carefully and comically worked out by Huck and Jim. One of Twain's best humorous statements, it takes only three paragraphs to outline. First Huck recounts running eight hours at night, swimming, now and then, catching fish, "kind of solemn, drifting down the big still river," lying on their backs, talking and occasionally chuckling in low tones to each other. Even as they pass St. Louis with its thousands of twinkling lights, there is no sound—the river is a special place, a holy churchlike place—even as early as chapter 12.

The discussion revolves around being "comfortable" about "borrowing." Huck slipped ashore nights and sometimes lifted a chicken that wasn't roosting comfortable. In *Pudd'nhead Wilson*, Twain would excuse the slave who lured a cold chicken to step onto a warm board and into his bag; his action was part of the natural outcome of slavery. In caricature morality, Huck reports, "Pap always said, take a chicken when you get a chance, because if you don't want him yourself you can easy find somebody that does, and a good deed ain't ever forgot." As with the Hank Bunker story, Huck detaches himself from Pap's statement, but its terms are both comic and appropriate. The presumption is that the self-centeredness of the frontiersman on the ownerless frontier becomes ironic humor in the settled areas where chickens are owned. The attachment of good deeds to theft, and the finding of someone else who needs help, carries forward the terms in which Huck prayed and got a fishline. Continuing to reason, Huck offers the concept of "borrowing" things as interpreted by the widow—just stealing. Since Jim is to be developed as a level-headed "nigger," he is allowed the resolution of the conflict between authorities: "the widow was partly right and pap was partly right," and so Huck and Jim agree not to borrow unripe fruit "because crabapples ain't ever good." Conflicts between authorities have set Huck and Jim free, and they accommodate themselves. Huck once again feels "comfortable," always a key word distinguishing freedom from authoritarian repression. Providing one more level of conflict between right and wrong, Twain develops his action through comedy toward the later climax—the crucial machinery of the novel is comic here, the achievement of Twain the deadpan ironic humorist.

A number of flamboyant elements dot chapters 12 through 19: the *Walter Scott* episode, reasoning on Sollermun and Frenchmen borrowed from a minstrel routine, the raftsmen chapter, Huck's first decision not to turn Jim in, the Grangerford–Shepherdson feud, and the entry of the Duke and Dauphin. The episodes are either reprises of the themes already developed or expansions of them pointing forward to even greater levels of spiritual development. The *Walter Scott* exemplifies Twain's method of compacting moral action within the comic irony of a melodramatic event—a method practiced in the character of Yokel and the robber gang in *The Prince and the Pauper* and in Morgan le Fay's dungeons in *A Connecticut Yankee* as well as in Huck's narrative.

As Huck and Jim get comfortable with their ethics about borrowing, they discover the sinking derelict steamboat *Walter Scott*. The use of the English romancer's name implicates southern romanticism, which Twain saw as a bankrupt tradition. She has "killed herself" on a rock and Jim is "dead against" landing. Huck forces the landing on the "mournful and lonesome" derelict by appeal to Tom Sawyer—recalling the essential feelings that Tom Sawyer engendered in Huck at the novel's opening, but altering their format. Huck might "borrow" something: seegars of the "rich" captain might be on board ... the landing is to be an "adventure," "for pie," with "style," and a chance to "spread" out in Sawyer fashion. Motives that had caused Tom to endanger Huck in the original joke on Jim are thus represented to the reader in Huck's actions, but with a radically expanded melodrama. Pointing forward in the novel, they also foreshadow the last fifth of the book.

LOUIS J. BUDD ON HISTORICAL RELEVANCE

For readers charmed by Huck's language, the period when the novel was written or even its stated time of action does not seem all that long ago. They slip back into a vanished river culture with warmer empathy than they can work up for the society of Lewis's *Main Street* or Dos Passos's *U.S.A.* Like *The Scarlet Letter* and *Moby-Dick*, the usual peers of *Huckleberry Finn* for those who nominate American masterpieces of the nineteenth century by threes, it has an exotic flavor. Yet it feels close to ordinary experience. Asserting the universality of a great classic for *Huckleberry Finn* does not explain enough. It not only rose out of a firm historical context, but it stands forth more sharply when seen against Twain's time and place and, in turn, makes them blindingly familiar.

Anybody who has tried to hone a sense of American history can migrate into Huck's world with special ease because of both the "frontier thesis" and the career of racism. Heightened for Twainians by DeVoto, the vision of the West as a haven of democracy, individualism, and pioneer ingenuity lives on. For a few romantics, escape to somewhere, as they take Huck to be proposing, is still possible. Likewise, the color-ridden, Faulknerian South and therefore the antebellum culture it descends from stick in our imagination. Actually, by 1885 the dominant North was already dominated by urbanism, technology, bureaucracy in industry as well as government, and machine politics. Twain protected himself from rigorous historians by giving the time of action vaguely as "forty to fifty years" earlier and avoiding unshakable clues like the name of a sitting president. Nevertheless, strangely but impressively, many later readers have assumed that *Huckleberry Finn* speaks to and about the society they are struggling through.

Those who claim historical accuracy or impact for it both

help and hurt its reputation misleadingly. It can get far too much credit for relevance in 1885 to an age of Wall Street barons, the rise of industrial and then banking monopolies, the recruiting for imperialism, and Populist militance in that same Mississippi Valley. Was there any territory left that Huck could escape to for long, ahead of the settlers and boomers?[12] To the extent that Twain himself doubted that possibility, we have to smile at Huck's plan as uninformed. Likewise, we need to decide how distinctly Twain wanted to draw a parallel with the situation of the emancipated slaves twenty years after the Civil War. The power brokers, having struck a deal after the election of 1876, were pushing the blacks toward their nadir in the first decade of the twentieth century. Does Jim essentially challenge the paternalism that Uncle Remus is happy to accept from Joel Chandler Harris, who admired the novel heartily? Some of Jim's descendants have started to attack its reputation for scorning racism, accepted even by Marxist critics, and in 1983 a black publisher, previously an administrator for a high school, edited out the word "nigger." Deservedly more influential, Ralph Ellison objects that "Jim's friendship for Huck comes across as that of a boy for another boy rather than as the friendship of an adult for a junior."[13]

An old critical question is whether it is possible to appreciate a novel properly without reentering the author's day-to-day context, which may be more compelling than the times written about when they are still more distant. An avid consumer of newspapers, Twain continually expressed topical attitudes. In his mind, the Grangerford–Shepherdson feud, to us apparently a purely antebellum touch, satirized a contemporary problem. Less insistently, his vignette of the "softy, soothering undertaker" projected a belief that ground burial had become archaic and unsanitary. Although the Tom Sawyer made foolish by romantic books stretched back to Don Quixote, he also served a then contemporary breed of double agents, of enemies within the gates. Many novelists were appeasing their middle-class audience with characters whose common sense—and, if women, their virginal caution—was muddled by reading fiction.

Inevitably, time develops another bothersome effect. If, like the reader-response critics, we hold that a novel exists only as it is being experienced by someone who thus becomes the author's collaborator, then its frame of reference shifts toward the moment whenever that process is occurring. A radical of the 1980s interacts with *Huckleberry Finn* differently even from such a prescient liberal as Randolph Bourne, who, well ahead of the intellectuals' contempt for the 1920s, perceived Twain as "reassuring every American in his self-complacency." On the other hand, Wilsonian idealism, so long as it lasted into that decade, could encourage Americans to admire Huck as both innocent and redemptive. The Great Depression, unexpectedly, taught some readers to romanticize Huck's kind of folks; as a publisher's blurb might say, if you liked Sandburg's *The People, Yes* (1936) and Steinbeck's *The Grapes of Wrath* (1939), you'd love *Huckleberry Finn*.

The context of literature also includes the history of the canon, that slowly changing roll of works that reach the summit of their genre and deserve any mission that the establishment can find for them.[14] Inescapably, the claims then validating the canon affected the early reactions to *Huckleberry Finn*. During the 1880s, the canon itself was reaching its high point of authority under Matthew Arnold's stern ideal of the best that had been thought and said by humankind. Many attacks on *Huckleberry Finn* applied a somewhat new principle; instead of belaboring novels in general, as they would have done a hundred or fifty years before, they scolded it as unworthy of its kind. When critics increasingly accepted it as worthy, they found reasons for proving that it satisfied the rules for a novel of lasting value after all. When they refined those rules into a sophisticated genre, they invoked symmetries of form to cover and even justify the political retreat that underlay Tom's toying with Jim in the Evasion sequence.

Notes

12. Roy Harvey Pearce, "'The End. Yours Truly, Huck Finn': Postscript," *Modern Language Notes* 24 (September 1963): 253–6,

speculates intriguingly and plausibly that Twain was alert to the latest territorial affairs.

13. "The Negro Writer in America: Change the Joke and Slip the Yoke," *Partisan Review* 25 (Spring 1958): 212–22.

14. For an admirable analysis, see Alvin B. Kernan, *The Imaginary Library: An Essay on Literature and Society* (Princeton, N.J.: Princeton University Press, 1982).

MICHAEL EGAN ON HUCK'S LANGUAGE CONVENTIONS

Twain involves us in Huck's circumstances so quickly (who is Aunt Polly? Mary? The dishonest Mr Mark Twain, etc.?) that we don't notice our more or less rapid entanglement in his vocabulary and speech rhythms. Yet by the end of the first paragraph we have already acquired a sense of Huck's repetitive lilt (a characteristic instance is the final sentence in the quotation) and have learned that the past tense of 'see' is 'seen'; and that 'without' can also mean 'excepting'. Our sense of English has already shifted and we are, linguistically speaking, off-balance and expectant. The process is so unobtrusively compelling that we soon accept the language conventions which later permit Huck's extraordinary grammatical transformations, in the Chomskyan sense, to sound perfectly natural and even logical: For example, when he disguises himself as a little girl and calls on Mrs Judith Loftus, he tells us how 'she got to talking about her husband, and about her relations up the river, and about how much better off they used to was ...' (Chapter 11). Extrapolated from the text it looks like a misprint; but in context it is barely noticeable. We have been taught to speak Finnian.

Elsewhere Huck plays havoc with past tenses, spawning adverbs, adjectives and verbs themselves with the neological abandon of a man inventing a whole new language. There is the 'cluttering' of bullfrogs on the river before dawn (Chapter 19), and the 'screaking' of a sweep in its lock as a raft is rowed by (Chapter 19). Frightened people 'skaddle' out of the reach of danger (Chapter 22), girls 'brisken' up a room, and when you steal something you 'smouch' it. In one of the novel's great scenes, the Wilks funeral (Chapter 27), an undertaker is described as having 'softy soothering ways', while a 'melodeum' at the back of the room sounds 'pretty skreeky' and colicky. The past tense of 'climb' is given, much more strongly, as 'clumb' and Jim, in his story about his deaf daughter, 'crope' instead of 'crept' towards her (Chapter 23).

Twain's inventiveness is almost unlimited, verging on a kind of poetry. One of the strengths of the passage describing the storm, for instance, is the sheer beauty of the language. Elsewhere Tom Sawyer, Huck tells us, is not the sort of boy to 'meeky' along in a timid fashion, while in yet another fine characterisation of the wind he speaks of the way it 'swished and swushed' by. As this example illustrates, Twain had deep sense of the onomatopoeic. Later he employs it to invent the vowel-less verb:

> Blamed if the king didn't have to brace up mighty :quick, or he'd a squshed down like a bluff bank that the river has cut under, it took him so sudden—and mind you, it was a thing that was calculated to make most *anybody* sqush ...
> (*Huckleberry Finn*, Chapter 29.)

Inventions like these enable him to import a kind of infectious irresponsibility into his prose, so that he can communicate things beyond the surface meanings of words themselves. Mrs Loftus's little solecism, for example, (how much better off they used to was); adds a further dimension to what we subsequently learn about the experience of poverty in the deep South at that time. The actual language of the poor tells us something about poverty itself. On a lighter note Twain is able to say things like this:

> The duke, he never let on he suspicioned what was up, but just went goo-gooing around, happy and satisfied, like a jug that's googling out buttermilk ...
> (*Huckleberry* Finn, Chapter 29.)

The humour, the vividness and the very Americanness of this moment are inseparable from Huck's capacity to make a past-tense verb out of 'suspicion' and to invent the outrageous simile that hinges on the non-existent participle, 'googling'. Its effectiveness, however, is undeniable.

The point is, of course, that Twain was not merely writing prose. He was recording the speech of a way of life. *Huckleberry Finn* is one of the most aural novels in the language, and in order for it to be so Twain had to depart from the polite cadences of educated grammar and take us into the sensuous unexpectedness of living words and forms. One has only to compare the stilted formality of the passage from *Tom Sawyer* given below with almost any example from *Huckleberry Finn*— for instance, the point at which Twain makes an intransitive verb out of 'dark'—'the sky was darking up'—and speaks of the lightning beginning to 'wink and flitter'—to be aware of the enormous narrative advance that has been achieved. Twain's success is to striking that Huck is finally able to make us co-conspirators in his subversion of our language. At one point he produces a memorable image of Mississippi night, glittering with the visual and tactile: 'Everything was dead quiet, and it looked late and *smelt* late.' And then, confident that he has us spell-bound: 'You know what I mean—I don't know the words to put it in.' It is the helpless resignation of a victor.

Twain's language in *Huckleberry Finn* is his most significant contribution to literature, comparable, in its of course considerably more modest way, to Chaucer's use of spoken English in *The Canterbury Tales* or Dante's use of Italian in the *Divina Commedia*. T.S. Eliot declared that Twain had 'purified the language of the tribe', and compared him in this respect with Swift and Dryden. He was 'one of those writers, of whom there are not a great many in literature, who have discovered a new way of writing, valid not only for themselves but for others.' ('American Literature and the American Language,' *Washington University Studies*, No. 23, St Louis, 1953, pp. 16–17.)

Twain's linguistic inventiveness apart, however, his commitment to what I earlier called the representative and the typical, in other words, to the truth of a given situation, is the major stylistic mode in *Huckleberry Finn*. The two innovations combine to make it the most important novel written in nineteenth century America. Moreover, as a literary device Twain's recourse to the aural and observable fact is not found elsewhere in his fiction in such consistent application, though of course it is the greatest strength of his travel books and other non-fiction studies. *Huckleberry Finn* thus anticipated what was to become a major characteristic of writing in the next century—the increased blurring of the distinction between documentary and fiction. In a wholly valid and legitimate way Twain's novel can be considered almost a dramatised casebook, a living study in geographic, political and sociological actuality which, when taken together, yield a supremely fine work of literary art.

WILLIAM R. EVERDELL ON THE AUTOBIOGRAPHICAL MODE OF NARRATION

No American who has read *Adventures of Huckleberry Finn* ever seems to have gotten over it. Ernest Hemingway thought that all modern American literature had come out of this one book, which is coming it strong; but this view is endorsed by nearly everyone who earns his livelihood in the burgeoning profession called Twain studies.[1] Hemingway's enthusiasm may well reflect the excitement of discovering Huck during his boyhood in Illinois (the book was thirteen years old when he was born); but T.S. Eliot pronounced *Huckleberry Finn* "a masterpiece," and Eliot, a decade older than Hemingway, had grown up in Twain's own Missouri without being allowed to make the same discovery.[2] As Twain remembered it, the Mississippi River "from end to end was flaked with coal-fleets and timber rafts;" while Eliot saw a "river with its cargo of dead Negroes, cows and chicken coops."[3] Of course, Twain went to Eliot's birthplace, "the crescent city" of Saint Louis, fairly often; but on his last visit in 1902 Eliot was fourteen, a day boy at a private school.[4] Walter Blair, who has brought to light so many of the novel's sources, wrote that "to imagine what would have happened to Eliot's work if he had been influenced by Mark Twain boggles the imagination."[5] It is my purpose here, nevertheless, to suggest that such an influence, however indirect and cultural, may be a central thread, so far largely unexamined, in that history so grandly summed up by Hemingway of modern American literature.[6]

The very first review of *Huckleberry Finn*, by T.S. Perry, seized on the book's "great advantage" (presumably over *Tom Sawyer*) "of being written in autobiographical form." The second, by Brander Matthews, delighted in having discovered Huck "from the inside."[7] Much of value has been written since on what this narrative point of view does for the depth and richness of the novel, its combination of simple truth and moral irony, its wonderful stew of precisely rendered dialects, its humor and pathos, and its perennial appeal to readers of all ages. What seems not to have been much written about, however, is first, how did the form arise and what were its uses at the time Twain made it his own; and second, how much did *Huckleberry Finn* contribute to the extraordinary vaudevillean destiny of first-person narrative in American (no less than European) literature of the twentieth century. In short, it may turn out that even Philip Rahv's redskin imagination boggles too easily when it boggles at the kinship of J. Alfred Prufrock and Huckleberry Finn.

First of all, we need to free ourselves from the limits of Perry's "autobiographical form." There is not much doubt, of course, that Huck is writing a book. Indeed, he remarks on the last page that if he'd known "what a trouble it was," he wouldn't have tackled it. Huck has read books too, and is a dead accurate speller, plausibly and phonetically misspelling only those words ("diseased" for "deceased" and "doxolojer" for "doxology") that go beyond his frontier reader's vocabulary.[8] Twain himself unambiguously described his new novel as Huck's "autobiography" in one of his 1876 letters to Howells.[9] Even so, it is clear from the first line that Huck's writing of this story is no more than a means for the telling of it, and that Twain has raised up Huck as a speaker from the first hint of a dialect spelling. Huck can deal with any accent common on the Mississippi, but he quickly gives up on the task of "imitating" the pastiche-class of the Dauphin's English.[10] Not long after, he fails to "imitate" the real "king's English" when the true Wilks brothers arrive from England.[11] These are fundamentally oral feats and Huck's failures are fundamentally performance failures. No wonder then that Huck pronounces French with an American accent, but it is quite a surprise that having got his French "jabber out of a book," he should then proceed to spell it with an oral accent, "Polly-vous-franzy" instead of the "Parlez-vous français," which (unless the book was a pronunciation manual) he would have to have seen on the page.[12] No, *Huckleberry Finn* is only secondarily an autobiography. What it is, first and foremost, is a comic monologue.

The comic monologue occupies a shifting place in the space of rhetorical possibilities. The most comprehensive writing on the subject is rather sharply divided among discussions of different literary forms.[13] Nevertheless, writers are less bound than critics by distinctions between soliloquy in the theater, narrative monologue in fiction, and monodrama, or even lyric, in poetry. Of course it makes a difference whether a text is written as a tale, a playing script, a torch song, or a diary, but there seems to be a spectrum which contains not only these but other possibilities.

(...)

Twain so enjoyed the misdirection required by a good joke that many critics have seen it as the heart of his character. He loved to risk a long silence or a moment of embarrassed misunderstanding leading up to a punch line, but he also thrived on the "artillery laughter" and applause."[39] In his capacity of platform humorist, Twain remained a true son of the performing frontier, and an uncomfortably close relation of the duke and the dauphin. The preparation was always more work than he let on. The performance-reading that he had seen Dickens do in 1867 turned out to be harder than the humorous lecture or even the toast. "I supposed it would be necessary to do like Dickens—get out on the platform and read from the book. I did that and made a botch of it."[40] Nevertheless, in the summer of 1884, the year *Huckleberry Finn* was published, he went on tour with George Washington Cable, reading from and performing his own work. The best work he had on hand that summer, and the easiest for him to perform, was *Huckleberry Finn*.[41]

It has been pointed out that the precursor of the comic monologue in America is the anecdote, or what is known here as the tall tale. The anecdote was certainly Twain's most common form, whether speaking or writing, and he told many of them in the first person, in many voices, including his own. First person was the rule for anecdotes, even though the story's teller is hardly ever the story's butt, and despite the misleading fact that the best early examples of anecdotes in print are rigidly framed as third-person fiction. Blair counts collections of "mock oral tales" like *Some Adventures of Captain Simon Suggs* (1845) and *Polly Peablossom's Wedding* (1851) as sources of Twain's material; but they should also be examined for traces of his form, American versions of the comic monologue.[42] The genteel written versions often obscure the immediacy of the authentic spoken version. "Written things are not for speech," said Twain, explaining how the performance version of one anecdote came to differ from the written one; "their form is literary; they are stiff, inflexible and will not lend themselves to happy and effective delivery with the tongue—where their purpose is to merely entertain, not instruct; they have to be broken up, colloquialized and turned into the common forms of unpremeditated talk."[43] Perhaps the purest example of a tall story in Twain's longer works is the quoted dialogue on alligators in *Life on the Mississippi*, but the best example of the autobiographical comic monologue, and the most sustained example of that form in his work, is undoubtedly *Huckleberry Finn*.[44]

Notes

1. Ernest Hemingway, *The Green Hills of Africa* (New York: Scribner's 1935), p. 22.

2. T.S. Eliot, preface to *Huckleberry Finn* (1930), rept. in Sculley Bradley et al., eds. *Adventures of Huckleberry Finn* (New York: Norton, 1977), p. 328.

3. Mark Twain, *Life on the Mississippi*, in *Mississippi Writings* (New York: Library of America, 1982), p. 239; T.S. Eliot, "The Dry Salvages," *The Complete Poems and Plays, 1909–1950* (New York: Harcourt, Brace, 1959), p. 133.

4. Twain, *Mississippi Writings*, p. 520.

5. Walter Blair, *Mark Twain and Huck Finn* (Berkeley: Univ. of California Press, 1960), pp. 6–7.

6. The research for this article was financed in 190–91 by a Wallace Foundation Teacher/Scholarship from the National Endowment for the Humanities. The author is grateful to colleagues Jane Avrich, Beth Bosworth, Laura Kennelly, and Nancy White for comments and criticism.

7. T.S. Perry and Brander Matthews, in Bradley, et al, eds., *Huckleberry Finn*, pp. 289, 292.

8. Twain, *Mississippi Writings*, p. 786.

9. Twain to Howells, August 9, 1876, in H.N. Smith and W.M. Gibson, eds., *Mark Twain-Howells Letters, 1872–1910*, Vol. 1 (Cambridge: Harvard Univ. Press, 1960), p. 144.

10. Twain, *Mississippi Writings*, p. 783.

11. Twain, *Mississippi Writings*, p. 816.

12. Twain, *Mississippi Writings*, p. 702.

13. Melvin Friedman, *Stream of Consciousness: A Study in Literary Method* (New Haven: Yale Univ. Press, 1955); Egbert Faas, *Poesie als Psychogramm: Die Dramatisch-monologische Versdichtung im Victorianischen Zeitalter* (Munich: Fink, 1974); A. Dwight Culler, "Monodrama and the Dramatic Monologue," *PMLA*, 90 (1975), 366–385; U. Fülleborn, "Literatur des 'Ich' and Literatur des 'Ist,'" in Fülleborn and M. Engel, eds., *Das neuzeitliche Ich in der Literatur des 18. und 20 Jahrhunderts* (Munich: Fink, 1988); Ralph R. Rader, "The Dramatic Monologue and Related Lyric Forms," *CritI*, 3 (1976), 131–51.

39. Twain, *Autobiography*, pp. 146, 181–82, 214, 310; Twain to Livy Clemens, November 14, 1879, in Albert Bigelow Paine, ed., *Mark Twain's Letters*, Vol. 1 (New York: Harper, 1917), p. 371.

40. Twain, *Autobiography*, p. 176.

41. Kaplan, *Mr. Clemens and Mark Twain*, pp. 302–04. One of Twain's platform pieces was Chapter 14 of *Huckleberry Finn*, which he titled "Sollermun." Twain wrote about touring with Cable in *Life on the Mississippi* and included a key scene from *Huckleberry Finn* in Chapter 3 of the finished book. See Twain, *Mississippi Writings*, p. 485; also Twain, *Autobiography*, pp. 176, 235–36.

42. Twain, *Adventures of Huckleberry Finn*, pp. 253–58; Blair, *Mark Twain and Huckleberry Finn*, p. 280; Walter Blair, *Native American Humor (1800–1900)* (New York: American Book, 1937), p. 89. Vance Randolph offered a collection of his material in 1976, but with the genteel third-person frame pushed back into the somewhat less misleading realm of sociology. Vance Randolph, ed., *Pissing in the Snow* (Urbana: Univ. of Illinois Press, 1976).

43. Twain, *Autobiography*, p. 176.

44. Twain, *Mississippi Writings*, pp. 372–77.

VICTOR A. DOYNO ON HUCK'S DISILLUSIONMENT WITH THE JUDEO-CHRISTIAN TRADITION

How quickly does the concern for morality and religion surface in the novel? We recall the initial references to an earlier novel and to the moral issues of lying and truth-telling:

> You don't know about me, without you have read a book by the name of "The Adventures of Tom Sawyer," but that ain't no matter. That book was made by Mr. Mark Twain, and he told the truth, mainly. There was things which he stretched, but mainly he told the truth. That is nothing. I never seen anybody but lied, one time or another, without it was Aunt Polly, or the widow, or maybe Mary.... (17)

The central concerns of Christianity and morality dominate the first chapter, with truth-telling, religious cliches such as "a poor lost lamb," and a grumbling grace over food. The widow attempts to indoctrinate Huck in the Judeo-Christian tradition by reading from the Bible the story of "Moses and the Bulrushers." Huck listens attentively perhaps because he at first thought the story involved people who charged at bulls, probably an eventful kind of story. Of course, the story actually deals, appropriately enough, with hereditary status, religion, an abandoned child on a water journey, and liberation from slavery. But Huck experiences two disillusionments: he learns that the story is not what he expected but concerns "dead people," and he quickly realizes that the widow's restrictions about tobacco are hypocritical and not based on experience.

Huck's direct conflict with books and with conventional religion occurs as Miss Watson criticizes Huck's behavior and warms to her subject. We can observe a contrast between her volubility and Huck's increasing reticence:

> Her sister, Miss Watson, a tolerable slim old maid, with goggles on, had just come to live with her, and took a set at me now, with a spelling-book. She worked me middling hard for about an hour, and then the widow made her ease up. I couldn't stood it much longer. Then for an hour it was deadly dull, and I was fidgety. Miss Watson would say, "Dont put your feet up there, Huckleberry;" and "dont scrunch up like that, Huckleberry—set up straight;" and pretty soon she would say, "Don't gap and stretch like that, Huckleberry—why don't you try to behave?" Then she told me all about the bad place, and I said I wished I was there. She got mad, then, but I didn't mean no harm. All I wanted was to go somewheres; all I wanted was a change, I warn't particular. She said it was wicked to say what I said; said she wouldn't say it for the whole world; *she* was going to live so as to go to the good place. Well, I couldn't see no advantage in going where she was going, so I made up my mind I wouldn't try for it. But I never said so, because it would only make trouble, and wouldn't do no good. (19)

Huck's behavior and attitude in the opening chapter correspond to Kohlberg's definition of the first stage of moral development, simple deference to a superior force or authority. Despite coercive predictive threats and, later, internalized fears about damnation in hell, Huck will create his own integrity; he will even become willing to go to hell. His autonomy develops as he learns to withhold his opinion, as he experiments with the adolescent habit of controlling the interaction or situation by his silence.

Repeatedly Huck's common sense and naive literalism combine with his perceptiveness to lead him to observe silliness in society. When he questions the tradition or rules of religion (or of Tom Sawyer's romantic fiction), Huck is branded as a fool. A countermotif develops, however, because frequently Huck is silent: "But I never said so." Accordingly, this fiction uses a contrast between Huck's reticence or inarticulate withdrawal from many other characters and his fluent revelations to the reader.

Huck submits himself to the civilizing influence at the widow's house only intermittently. Prior to the novel's opening he had "lit out," and he takes another chance to leave, temporarily, that first evening for some adventures with Tom. But when he returns he reveals a more complex response to each adult's reactions. To Miss Watson, who treats him harshly, he reacts in a way which shows an instrumentalist-functionalist view of the world (Kohlberg's second stage); but to the disappointed widow, who treats him kindly, he reacts by attempting to be good:

Well, I got a good going-over in the morning, from Old Miss Watson, on account of my clothes; but the widow she didn't scold, but only cleaned off the grease and clay and looked so sorry that I thought I would behave a while if I could. Then Miss Watson she took me in the closet and prayed, but nothing came of it. She told me to pray every day, and whatever I asked for I would get it. But it warn't so. I tried it. Once I got a fish-line, but no hooks. It warn't any good to me without hooks. I tried for the hooks three or four times, but somehow I couldn't make it work. By-and-by, one day, I asked Miss Watson to try for me, but she said I was a fool. She never told me why, and I couldn't make it out no way.

> I set down, one time, back in the woods, and had a long think about it. I says to myself, if a body can get anything they pray for, why don't Deacon Winn get back the money he lost on pork? Why can't the widow get back her silver snuff box that was stole? Why can't Miss Watson fat up? No, says I to myself, there ain't nothing in it. (29)

Huck tries these prayers because of a practical need, attempting as a naive literalist to make a new trick work and expressing his needs in short simple sentences. His rational thoughts about other persons' prayers reveal a prescient skepticism. Huck may subconsciously calculate that a Deacon's Winn's prayers just lose, although they ought to be more effective than the average person's.[6] The final devastating proof of the inefficacy of prayer occurs in the combination of personal and material concern in the animal terminology of Miss Watson's inability to "fat up."

The next step in Huck's progress appears as he turns to the kindly parental figure, the widow:

> I went and told the widow about it, and she said the thing a body could get by praying for it was "spiritual gifts." This was too many for me, but she told me what she meant—I must help other people, and do everything I could for other people, and look out for them all the time, and never think about myself. This was including Miss Watson, as I took it. I went out in the woods and turned it over in my mind a long time, but I couldn't see no advantage about it—except for the other people—so at last I reckoned I wouldn't worry about it any more, but just let it go. (29–30)

As we shall see repeatedly, Huck's ability to see things from another person's point of view is crucial to his developing character, to his sympathy, to his morality. Ultimately, Huck does come to have "spiritual gifts," because he unselfishly attempts "good works," trying to help the robbers on the Winter Scott, the Wilks girls, the king and duke, and, most importantly, Jim. Huck's intuitive kindness and decency grow to become dominant parts of his personality—parts which are in clear conflict with the actual observed practices of the conventional Christians.

The conflict between two attitudes toward religion appears to Huck:

> Sometimes the widow would take me one side and talk about Providence in a way to make a body's mouth water; but maybe next day Miss Watson would take hold and knock it all down again. I judged I could see that there was two Providences, and a poor chap would stand considerable show with the widow's Providence, but if Miss Watson's got him there warn't no help for him any more. I thought it all out, and reckoned I would belong to the widow's, if he wanted me, though I couldn't make out how he was agoing to be any better off then than what he was before, seeing I was so ignorant and so kind of low-down and ornery. (30)

Amusingly, Huck thinks about the two Providences rather as he would about two rival gangs.[7] Characteristically, Huck does not abase himself before a god-figure, but attempts to think *from* each Providence's point of view, calculating what he would add to the side. Such an implied equality of Huck's personality and Providence helps the novel appeal to a nation with democratic, practical, individualistic values. In the early chapters, prayer, Sunday school, and religion appear as children's games; Huck's effort to summon a genie works no more successfully than the prayer for fish hooks. The attempt to rob a caravan of rich Arabs smacks of bookish romance, but the robbery actually attacks a Sunday school picnic. Praying and playing actually involve similar fantasizing, both based upon unrealistic bookish authorities. Even Pap Finn's brief reformation includes attention to both bookishness ("turn over a new leaf" and signing his pledge) and history ("the holiest time on record"). Of course, his religious reformation fails.

Notes

6. Some adults retain this instrumentalist view; Twain mentioned a "Church of the Holy Speculators."

7. Also see Edgar Branch's treatment in *The Literary Apprenticeship of Mark Twain* 199, et seq.

EVERETT EMERSON ON THE COMPLEXITY OF HUCK'S CHARACTER

As Mark Twain's most richly conceived fictional creation, Huckleberry Finn exhibits a complex set of traits. He is an innocent, but with the exception of a few blind spots he is instinctively shrewd and far from naive. His resourceful imagination helps him to survive even though he has as his companion an escaping slave. He has fundamental convictions, which deepen as the book continues, in opposition to those of the society in which he is placed. His most meaningful attitudes are based on an acute moral apprehension. Because Huck is intelligent, quick, and inventive, he is able to survive, but because he is lower-class, without education or status, he is powerless to accomplish much. (Mark Twain's later hero, the Connecticut Yankee, shows what a hero *with* power could do, but most readers in our time have been appalled by what the Yankee awesomely accomplishes.) Huck's age is, as the author might say, slippery. He is fourteen but prepubescent; sometimes capable beyond his years, he seems often much younger than fourteen. He has no family—or worse than none, since his father is at best a parasite, at worst a sinister and sadistic alcoholic. But Huck's imagination conjures up sentimental stories in which he joins a close-knit family. He is ungrammatical, but he can spell—after a fashion. Most readers do not find themselves reading a book but listening to a skillful talker. Like his creator, who relished amateur playacting, Huck can assume a role with finesse and satisfaction. He is a nonconformist, partly by inclination and partly by ignorance. At the opening of the book, he is just starting to grasp, and largely to dislike, the ways of civilization. A pleasure-seeker, he nevertheless makes tough moral decisions. He has wide-open eyes; he is always alert, aware. Perhaps most magnetically, he is oblivious to his own worth—not modest or self-effacing but simply profoundly obtuse. As a narrator, Huck makes extensive use of a technique Mark Twain had developed early: telling not so much what happens as what was experienced, by the ear, the eye, all the senses. Occasionally Huck addresses the reader intimately, telling him almost privately what his senses make him feel.

Huck's reliability as a narrator and his appealing personality establish the central conflict of the book, which is not so much between Huck and his society as between Huck and himself. Throughout his adventures, Huck has an excruciating struggle that recalls the more amusing and more physical one between Mark Twain and his conscience in "The Carnival of Crime in Connecticut" (1876). Huck has been brought up in a slaveholding society that reinforced the basis of its peculiar institution by appeals to religious authority, especially that of the Bible. Victimized by this thorough indoctrination, Huck is able to help his friend Jim escape from slavery only by believing himself to be depraved. In chapter 31, Huck states his belief that "if I was to ever see anybody from that town [St. Petersburg] again, I'd be ready to get down and lick his boots for shame." In a notebook entry of 1895, Mark Twain refers to *Huckleberry Finn* in such a way as to suggest the centrality of Huck's struggle, writing of his belief in "the proposition that in a crucial moral emergency a sound heart is a safer guide than an ill-trained conscience. I sh'd support this doctrine from a book of mine where a sound heart & a deformed conscience come into collision & conscience suffers defeat. Two persons figure in this chapter: Jim, a middle-aged slave, & Huck Finn, a boy of 14, son of the town drunkard. These two are close friends, bosom friends, drawn together by community of misfortune."[14]

Huck Finn is not Mark Twain, but he nonetheless resembles the writer's identification of himself as both the innocent *and* the veteran. Huck displays his innocence when he himself is hoodwinked. He visits a circus and is taken in by a horseback rider whose cavortings give him a real scare. But mostly through Huck the writer was able to explore two intertwined themes that engaged him fully: the relationship of the individual to society, and the meaning of freedom. (In a late fragment, "Indiantown" [1899], Mark Twain was to suggest strongly that he had a bad conscience over his having won a shaky place in eastern society—by becoming a hypocrite.) Although Huck (like Melville's Confidence Man) wears a variety of masks and identities in order to survive, he never sacrifices his fundamental honesty. He skillfully copes with society, even that of the feudal and feuding Grangerfords, without losing his humanity; in fact, he becomes more human and achieves a stronger individualistic identity. He and Jim are most fully themselves on the raft, away from society's oppressions, as Huck insists at the end of chapter 18: "Other places do seem so cramped up and smothery, but a raft don't. You feel mighty free and easy and comfortable on a raft."

The writer and most readers approve of Huck's being an outsider, apart from a society dominated by sentimentalism, vulgarity, cruelty, and dying religion. The fact that Huck feels obliged to look up to Tom as an authority figure is powerfully ironic, since Huck's innate attitudes and actions provide a severe judgment on Tom. The best parts of the book are devoted to Huck's disenchantment with Tom and his artificial ways, Huck and Jim's comradeship on the raft, and Huck's celebration of freedom and nature. The reader and the writer know that one day the raft will have to tie up, that Huck will have to return to a less isolated condition. Although he fantasizes about how he will "light out for the Territory," in none of the sequels can the author show Huck exercising his freedom: he ends up back again with Tom, once more looking up to him. There is no way for him to achieve self-fulfillment, for his creator was unable to conceive a setting that would permit the expansion of his consciousness. Huck is free, but has no place to go. He cannot grow up. Thus it has been argued that Huck's "function ... is to demonstrate the absolute incompatibility of the sort of self he is and the sort of world in which he tries so hard to live."[15] Although Huck is a fully realized character whose tale is masterfully told, the seriousness of his continuing debate with his conscience concerning what to do with Jim is undercut by the fact that the writer used Huck simultaneously as a deadpan comic mask, as in the circus episode. Moreover, if Huck is to be understood as an innocent hero confronting evil, then his inner life is too simple for him to play a truly tragic role.[16]

Notes

14. *Huckleberry Finn* (1988), p 806.

15. Pearce, "Yours truly, Huck Finn;," in *One Hundred Years of "Huckleberry Finn,"* ed. Sattelmeyer and Crowley, p. 314.

16. My comments here are indebted to H. N. Smith, *Democracy and the Novel*, pp. 105–14, and Trachtenberg, "The Form of Freedom in *Adventures of Huckleberry Finn.*"

GEORGE C. CARRINGTON, JR. ON THE UNITY OF *HUCKLEBERRY FINN*

In one sense *Huckleberry Finn* is situations and dramas, but in another sense it is some kind of a whole. Clearly it is not a well-articulated structure in the Aristotelian sense—only a few of the dramas, like Pokeville, and the Nonesuch, are that—but even if it lacks such a structure, it does begin, it does have a middle section, and it does stop. That sounds like a parody of traditional literary form, and indeed it is one of Twain's aims to deny the reader the comforts of conventional form, to make him experience chaos along with the characters, and thus to make him accept drama as the characters do. I will discuss below the reader's experience of the book. Before looking at *Huckleberry Finn* from outside as the reader sees it, it is necessary to look at what on the inside makes it a whole—that is, to look at Huck as the narrator.

In this novel about a turbulent situational world it is Huck whose presentation and embodiment of it provide the only continuity. The formal qualities of Huck the presenter dominate and determine the archetypal qualities of Huck the embodiment of traits, as the opening and closing paragraphs of the novel suggest. At the beginning Huck shows himself aware of a subtle but major problem of presentation, that of the dependence of truth-telling on precision: "'The Adventures of Tom Sawyer' was made by Mr. Mark Twain, and he told the truth, mainly. There was things which he stretched, but mainly he told the truth.... It is mostly a true book, with some stretchers, as I said before" (chap. 1). Huck is a conscious, concerned narrator, and he knows that he is doing something special and final. At the end, after what we can take to be a sustained effort to tell the truth and avoid "stretchers," Huck is relieved: "So there ain't nothing more to write about, and I am rotten glad of it, because if I'd a knowed what a trouble it was to make a book I wouldn't a tackled it and ain't agoing to no more" (Chap. the Last). And Huck never did; Twain never did use him again in a major, serious work of fiction.[1]

When Howells observed that *Huckleberry Finn* was a "romance" because Huck was made able to tell his story,[2] he sensed that Twain was not writing local color or escapism but creating an unusual artistic strategy and a problem that draws attention to the strategy. The first-person narrator is inherently a distancing device.[3] Huck can offer us none of the "guidance" for which Wayne Booth prays in difficult fictional situations.[4] It is not that Huck is distant or fails to discuss problems. He often confides in "you," with whom he assumes he has a good deal in common, but he fails to clarify basic problems and pursue implications. Why is he so concerned about "stretchers"? Why, after learning through experience the difficulties of writing a book, does he continue to the end?

In working toward answers to these questions, it is necessary to keep in mind that Huck is the maker of the book. It is easy to forget or to ignore this point, thanks to Twain's guile. The novel is written at the Phelps house while Tom is recovering from his wound during a period of a few weeks after the evasion. There is only the one brief reference to the writing of the book itself ("there ain't nothing more to write about"), and that reference is followed and dominated by Huck's grumblings about the general difficulties of writing books. One is led to remember the difficulty of writing and forget the fact of writing. The short interval between Huck's experiences and his writing makes impossible the reflective passages and even the general air of contemplation that stamp a book long-considered (by the narrator) and then "done," like those other first-person American classics, *Moby-Dick* and *The Great Gatsby*. The opening of *Huckleberry Finn* is not suggestive of Huck's role as maker either. "Me" appears in the opening line, but with reference to Huck the character in *The Adventures of Tom Sawyer*, not Huck the writer living after the events of *Huckleberry Finn*. The writer discussed in the opening paragraph is Twain, not Huck. The word "Huck" does not appear until the sixth paragraph, where Huck is brought in not as a writer or narrator but as a passive character squirming in the clutches of Miss Watson. The full name "Huck Finn" does not appear until chapter 2.

The novel begins with such subtlety that it is almost impossible, especially in normal non-critical reading, to realize the shift from reflection and summary to the actual narrative itself. After commenting on *The Adventures of Tom Sawyer* in the first paragraph, Huck summarizes its ending in the second paragraph, and then, in the third, begins to summarize the post–*Tom Sawyer* events—that is, the events of *Huckleberry Finn*—in such a way that no one who had not read *Tom Sawyer* could tell which events are which. The paragraph shift is a signal, and to be sure Huck opens the book with a warning— "You don't know about me without you have read a book by the name of 'The Adventures of Tom Sawyer'"—but Huck follows that with the disarming comment, "but that ain't no matter." The summary-exposition of the third paragraph ("the old thing commenced again") leads to the details of what was wrong with the widow's typical meal, and a general comment, in the present tense, on the right kind of meal. We are apparently still in the area of the general, but now a new paragraph begins: "After supper she got out her book and learned me about Moses and the Bulrushers...." Without warning and thus without thought we have moved from the static general past to the dynamic immediate present, the present of fiction, in which the book remains until the last paragraph of Chapter the Last. Twain thus interlocks (1) general past, (2) general timeless present, and (3) specific fictional present.

Notes

1. Twain tried to use Huck in the unfinished "prairie-manuscript," and did use him in *Tom Sawyer Detective* and *Tom Sawyer Abroad*, neither of which add any dimensions to Huck or indeed have much literary quality. The prairie-manuscript has been edited by Walter Blair and published in *Life*, 20 December 1968, pp. 32A–50A, and in *Hannibal, Huck, and Tom* (Berkeley: University of California Press, 1969), pp. 81–140. Blair thinks that Twain dropped the story because he was unable to deal with a rape to which his narrative had become committed. But the story was going nowhere, and if it had had any vitality, Twain's fertile mind would never have been utterly defeated by a narrative block of the sort Blair discusses.

2. *Harper's Weekly* 41 (13 February 1897): 155. Howells was reviewing the first five volumes of Harper's Uniform Edition of Twain's works. Note Howells's respectful discussion of "romance" in *Criticism and Fiction*.

3. A.A. Mendilow, *Time and the Novel* (London: Peter Nevill, 1952), pp. 106 ff.

4. *The Rhetoric of Fiction* (Chicago: University of Chicago Press, 1961), pp. 187 ff.

LELAND KRAUTH ON THE CONVERGENCE OF SOUTHWESTERN HUMOR AND SENTIMENTALITY

Twain's humor invades and disrupts the central value systems and institutions of his time—and ours. It problematizes religion, manners, morals, society, culture, race, class, gender, and, ultimately, individual identity itself. Twain himself probably grasped the subversive power of his novel only slightly, enjoying its composition on forbidden Sundays and anticipating that some readers would dislike it. But, working through the mask of Huck, he freed himself more than ever before (and more than he ever would again) to sport with the world as he knew it, to laugh it, sometimes gently, sometimes violently, to smithereens. The humor of this book is liberated, for with differing degrees of severity it breaks taboo after taboo. Such transgression was no doubt the source of both the joy and the obsession Twain felt as he composed. The book itself is also liberating, for as it deploys humor to trample conventions, it draws its readers into complicity with its violations. It is no wonder that various readers at different times have recoiled from *Huck Finn*, finding it vulgar, or irreligious, or racist, or sexist, finding it, in short, objectionable in one way or another. And it is no wonder that those who embrace the book have often defended it by not taking its humor seriously. *Huck Finn* is, in Cox's perceptive phrase, "a hard book to take" (386).

But Mark Twain is not a nihilist. Despite the corrosive force of his humor, he struggles toward affirmation. Like a typical Victorian as he doubts the truth of religion, the validity of manners, the efficacy of wealth, the adequacy of traditional morality, the authenticity of culture, and the stability of identity, he nonetheless longs to ground life on some bedrock. To vary slightly Hawthorne's famous explanation of Melville's metaphysical dilemma, Twain can neither believe nor accept his disbelief. Even as his humor destabilizes the familiar world, creating what George C. Carrington Jr. has called a universe of "disorder" and "turbulence" (see chap. 1), Twain tries to reestablish an ethical order. He does so by writing a sentimental melodrama of the heart.

Despite its reputation as a major text of American realism, *Huck Finn* is actually something of a potboiler.[2] Certainly its main events—Pap's imprisonment of Huck, Huck's escape, the encounter with the cutthroat thieves on the *Walter Scott*, the feud, the shooting of Boggs, the facedown between Sherburn and the mob, the attempt to defraud the Wilks girls, and the final effort to steal Jim out of slavery—are all sensational. The plot of an innocent boy helping a kindly slave is worthy of Harriet Beecher Stowe. And then there is the enveloping atmosphere of terror. Hamlin Hill has concluded that fear was the "controlling emotion" of Twain's life (*God's Fool* 269), and whatever the truth of this, Twain makes fear the dominant emotion in Huck's experience. Huck is always threatened by something or someone. The novel is rife with dangers and dark plottings; it is driven by the ferocious and the sinister. Twain's presentation of emotion is often as exaggerated as the events that generate it. Feeling is insistently magnified, whether joyful—"It most killed Jim a—laughing" (*HF* 168)—or fearful—"it most scared the livers and lights out of me" (*HF* 259). Twain's sensationally episodic, emotion-filled thriller transpires in—and is unified by—a universe that is radically polarized, a universe of melodrama of the kind he imagined in *The Prince and the Pauper*.

Melodrama habitually envisions a world of stark, radically simplistic antitheses, a universe in which moral right and wrong, good behavior and bad, the socially responsible and the socially corrupt, the individually authentic, and the individually false, are projected as obvious, inevitable oppositions constitutive of life itself. *Huck Finn* is imagined in such terms. Of the many polarizations Twain's melodramatic imagination creates, perhaps the most important is the dichotomy between the manly and the feminine. Now that the original text has been fully restored in the California edition, this fundamental opposition is most evident in the contrast between the burly raftsmen and the delicate Emmeline, a contrast highlighted by their juxtaposition in chapters 16 and 17.

There is something slightly unreal about Huck's encounter with each. He observes the raftsmen for only a short time, and he knows Emmeline only through her family, her painting, and her poetry. Yet the two have a presence in the novel that exceeds Huck's experience of them. Twain presents them with such clarity and intensity, with such comic force, that they become as indelible in the novel as they were basic to his own imagining. At the deepest level, the contrast he draws between them no doubt arises from the impress of Clemens's parents, his compassionate, emotional mother, and his coldhearted, threatening father.[3] But the differences he creates also reflect the divergent worlds he had lived in: most recently, the sphere of domesticity, of the morally civilized and the culturally refined; earlier, the realm of the frontier, of the ethically wild and the culturally crude. Deep in Twain, these oppositions give structure to his novel. He presents their representatives as comic caricatures, of course, but his burlesque does not negate their function as normative counters. (Burlesque is, after all, a way of participating in what one mocks.) The world of Huck's enforced adventuring vibrates between the extremes they embody.

Twain draws the essential contrasts starkly: Emmeline is melancholy; the raftsmen are jubilant (they jump up and crack their heels); she is morbid; they are fecund; she is vulnerable; they are invincible; she is tender; they are tough. She simpers; they swagger. Both perform. And the postures assumed in each case, as well as their accompanying emotions, are palpably bogus (though their falsity is largely lost on Huck). Twain dramatizes here conflicting modes of self-identifying discourse—soft-talk versus tall-talk, the sentimental as opposed to the sadistic—which bespeak profound aesthetic, moral, and ontological differences. To the extent that these oppositions have a common basis in a preoccupation with death, the one lamenting it, the other threatening it, Twain seems to suggest that the entire culture is moribund. It is, dying because its capacity for authentic feeling has atrophied.

In varying degrees the gendered attitudes and attributes staged in Huck's encounters with the raftsmen and Emmeline inform and define all the other characters in the novel. On one side of the Great Gender Divide, the Widow Douglas, who never says a word in the book, is reported to call Huck a "poor lost lamb" (*HF* 2), a misconstruction of his character and circumstance conversant with Emmeline's sentimentality, and clearly Aunt Sally is gripped by excessive emotionality. On the other side of the Divide, Colonel Sherburn sadistically guns down Boggs and then announces his prowess in terms extravagant enough to match the raftsmen's brags: "Why, a man's safe in the hands of ten thousand of your kind" (*HF* 190).

2. Sundquist provides a useful overview of old and new approaches to realism (3–24). For specific commentary on *Huck Finn*, see Bell (39–69) and Quirk (83–105). Bell in particular challenges the idea that the novel is realistic, but his terms are quite different from mine here.

3. Clemens's remembrance of his father as austere and intimidating is documented in chapter 1; for his fond recollection of his mother as emotional and compassionate, see "Jane Lampton Clemens," *AI* 82–92. The various versions of the autobiography also draw the same contrasts.

RICHARD POIRIER ON GAMES AND TRICKERY AS SELF-EXPRESSION

More than any other novelist in English, Jane Austen is supremely confident that the appetite of her audience as well as of her characters can be satisfied by social unions, especially by marriage. It is not surprising that Emerson, Mark Twain, and Henry James should find "the pressure of appetite" unsatisfied. Despite the many differences among them, they all tend to see a necessary division between a part of us expressed by accommodations to social systems, and another, more admirable, even if impractical part, that exists in the imagination only, or in a vocabulary of abstractions, or in relation ships to landscape. Emerson has suffered from a general modern naïveté about romantic writers—the assumption that they are not aware of the incompatibility of many of their images with social and physical realities and with the inescapable pressures of time. Emerson was explicitly and eloquently aware of these tensions and of their result in what he called "doubleness." Huck Finn will later worry about "playing double," and to read Emerson with such novels in mind as the Leather-Stocking series, *Huckleberry Finn*, *The Portrait of a Lady*, or even *The Ambassadors*, where social artifice is given some positive definitions, is to come upon passages that describe the problem faced by the leading characters in these books and by their creators. The problem is that at some point, usually at the end, the heroes and heroines tend to escape definition in the social or even psychological terms on which, only to a lesser extent than in *Emma*, the novels themselves have depended. The eccentricities in the structure of *Huckleberry Finn* and in many of James's novels are thus symptoms of some larger distrust of social structures themselves. Emerson's phrasing is relevant to such works precisely because it is so general. Generality and vagueness are necessary attributes of all that is opposed to the fixed, publicly accredited reality of things as they are. Emerson's language is, if anything, less vague, less general, however, than most explanations of why, say, Huck must at the end of his novel "light out for the Territory" or why, at the end of hers, Isabel Archer must return to Rome. For Emerson,

> The worst feature of this double consciousness is, that the two lives, of the understanding and of the soul, which we lead, really show very little relation to each other; never meet and measure each other: one prevails now, all buzz and din; and the other prevails then, all infinitude and paradise; and, with the progress of life, the two discover no greater disposition to reconcile themselves. Yet, what is my faith? What am I? What but a thought of serenity and independence, an abode in the deep blue sky? Presently the clouds shut down again; yet we retain the belief that this pretty web we weave will at last be overshot and reticulated with veins of the blue, and that the moments will characterize the days. Patience, then, is for us, is it not? Patience, and still patience. When we pass, as we presently shall, into some new infinitude, out of this Iceland of negations, it will please us to reflect that though we had few virtues or consolations, we bore with our indigence, nor once strove to repair it with hypocrisy or false heat of any kind.

To claim that one can be a "thought of serenity and independence" is to claim the "freedom" imagined and lost in *Huckleberry Finn*, in Melville, above all in James, who is obsessed with the term. But praise of "patience," with such stoical iteration and even with a kind of pathetic call for reassurance—"Patience, then, is for us, is it not? Patience, and still patience"—is a recognition that there are in this life no very permanent lodgings in "the deep blue sky," at James's Gardencourt, or on the raft. Emerson's romanticism is the more impressive because, like James's, it is meant to relieve rather than merely elude the tensions of existence. Both insist, as William James was also to do, that to lack faith or belief is to be the reverse of worldly and practical, and that despite any contrary immediate evidence there are ultimate, practical benefits to the self from an active commitment to ideals. "This pretty web we weave will at last," Emerson persists in hoping, "be overshot and reticulated with veins of the blue." Such a hope, and not merely the "freedom" promised by death, turns "patience" into a form of action, of evolution.

The illusion that society might someday, somehow be transformed by the vision and sacrifice of an Isabel Archer or the needs of a Huck Finn is necessarily among the things that their creators try to make the reader believe even when they themselves are skeptical. It is part of the suspense, part of the beguilement, part even of the entertainment of fiction. The humor of Huck's narrative voice, the youthful glamour of Isabel's pronouncements in *The Portrait of a Lady*, the very ingenuousness of which makes us feel an amused tenderness for her—these result from styles meant to sustain us past the glowerings of our own knowledge about probable failure. Thereby, we can share in the nostalgic regret when the failures do occur, as if for a lost possibility. There is no better description of how we should read novels of this kind than that provided by Emerson, for whom the act of reading was itself an exercise of "double consciousness": "An imaginative book," he remarks in "The Poet," "renders us more service at first, by stimulating us through its tropes, than afterwards when we arrive at the precise sense of the author."

Slavery in Hannibal may not have been "the brutal plantation
article," but it was slavery nonetheless, with the all too familiar
mix of pain and powerlessness. Emma Knight of Hannibal was
born a slave near Florida, Missouri, Mark Twain's birthplace.
When she and her sisters outgrew the shoes their master gave
them only once a year, they had to go barefoot. "Our feet
would crack open from de cold and bleed. We would sit down
and bawl and cry because it hurt so," she told an interviewer
years after freedom had come. Her family had been separated,
her father sold at auction—and not simply to settle an estate.
"My father was took away. My mother said he was put upon a
block and sold 'cause de master wanted money to buy
something for de house." Clay Smith, another slave from
Hannibal, recalled that her aunt Harriet "was sold on de block
down on Fourth Street right here in Hannibal."

The slave trading at Melpontian Hall—about four blocks
from the house where the Clemens family lived—was so
repugnant to the Moores, a newly arrived family in town, that
they packed up and moved back to Wisconsin after a very brief
stay. Yet the disdain in which the citizens of Hannibal allegedly
held the slave trader was not so strong as to dissuade them
from using Melpontian Hall as their voting place on election
day.

All slaves were vulnerable to being sold away from friends
and family. Indeed, as Twain tells us, his own father was
responsible for one such sale, having exiled a slave named
Charley "from his home, his mother, and his friends, and all
things and creatures that make life dear." In 1842 John
Marshall Clemens, who had received the slave in settlement of
a long-standing debt, took Charley with him on a trip to collect
$470 he was owed by a man in Mississippi. John Clemens
found the financial trials of the Mississippi man so moving that
he "could not have the conscience" to collect the debt (as he
wrote home). But he had no qualms about selling Charley
down the river for about forty dollars' worth of tar—the same

amount that the king and the duke got for Jim when they sold him in the novel Twain would write some forty years later.

That the Deep South held no monopoly on cruelty as far as slaves were concerned is clear from Twain's own recollections. At age ten, in 1845, on one of Hannibal's main streets, he had watched a white master strike and kill a slave with a piece of iron, a memory that came back to him in Bombay. "I knew the man had a right to kill his slave if he wanted to, and yet it seemed a pitiful thing and somehow wrong, though why wrong I was not deep enough to explain.... Nobody in the village approved of that murder, but of course no one said much about it." On another occasion he recalled the community's response to the death of a slave at the hands of a white overseer: "Everybody seemed indifferent about it as regarded the slave—though considerable sympathy was felt for the slave's owner, who had been bereft of valuable property by a worthless person who was not able to pay for it." (The jarring intrusion of the fact that the murder of the slave left the owner "bereft of valuable property" resonates with the dry denouement of *Pudd'nhead Wilson*: "Everybody granted that if 'Tom' were white and free it would be unquestionably right to punish him—it would be no loss to anybody; but to shut up a valuable slave for life—that was quite another matter. As soon as the Governor understood the case, he pardoned Tom at once, and the creditors sold him down the river.")

Although the white citizens of Hannibal may have persuaded themselves that their "mild domestic slavery" was more humane than "the brutal plantation article," the efforts of slaves to escape at great personal risk and the fears of their owners that they would succeed belie the view that "as a rule our slaves were convinced and content." Emma Knight recalled her mistress's efforts to intimidate the slaves: "Mistress always told us dat if we run away somebody would catch and kill us. We was always scared when somebody strange come." Clay Smith recalled that "Father run away to Illinois during the war and we ain't never saw him again." Twain recalled from his early childhood in Florida, Missouri, hearing the "loud and frequent groans" of a runaway slave brought into the town "by six men who took him to an empty cabin, where they threw him on the floor and bound him with ropes." In 1847, when Twain was eleven, a runaway slave who belonged to a man named Neriam Todd swam across the river and hid in the swampy thickets of Sny Island, on the Illinois side of the Mississippi. A boy of Twain's acquaintance, Benson Blankenship, found him and brought him scraps of food instead of giving him up for a reward. (His behavior would become a model for aspects of Huck's behavior in *Huckleberry Finn*.) Some woodchoppers chased the slave into a part of the swamp called Bird Slough, where he disappeared; several days later, Sam Clemens and a few of his friends who had crossed the river to fish and hunt for berries found the slave's mutilated body. Yet courage persisted in the face of cruelty and danger. Indeed, slaves escaped with just enough frequency that insurance companies advertised policies to help protect slave owners from the financial loss involved.

* * *

There was something else the slaves had that pain and powerlessness and poverty didn't manage to extinguish: a rich and creative oral tradition. A young Sam Clemens who as yet knew nothing of his future calling listened to it every chance he got. The slaves didn't tell this attentive little white boy how much they suffered: stories like those Emma Knight and Clay Smith shared with interviewers years after slavery ended were not for his ears. What they did let him hear were ghost stories and satirical orations so masterfully constructed and delivered that he would remember them all his life.

Notes
77. *the brutal Plantation article* Twain, "Jane Lampton Clemens," posthumously published memoir in *HHT*, 49. See also the following general studies of slavery: *MBH*, 8–62; Harrison A. Trexler, *Slavery in Missouri, 1804–1865* (Baltimore: Johns Hopkins University Press, 1914); David A. March, "Slavery and Politics," in *The History of Missouri* (New York: Lewis Historical Publishing, 1967), 1: 810–36;

Emil Oberholzer, "The Legal Aspects of Slavery in Missouri," *Bulletin of the Missouri Historical Society* 6 (Jan. 1950): 540–45; W. Sherman Savage, "Contest over Slavery Between Illinois and Missouri," *Journal of Negro History* 28 (July 1943): 311–45.

77. *Our feet would crack open* Former slave Emma Knight, 924 North Street, Hannibal, Missouri; Western Historical Manuscripts Collection, University of Missouri, Columbia; rpt. in *The American Slave; A Composite Autobiography*. Supplement, series i. Volume 2: *Arkansas, Colorado, Minnesota, Missouri, and Oregon and Washington Narratives*, edited George P. Rawick, Contributions in Afro-American and African Studies, 35 (Westport: Greenwood Publishing, 1977), 202.

77. *was sold on de block* Former slave Clay Smith, 612 Butler Street, Hannibal, Missouri; Western Historical Manuscripts Collection, University of Missouri, Columbia; rpt. in *The American Slave*, 263.

77. *The slave trading at Melpontian Hall* Hagood and Hagood, "Hannibal's Underground Railroad," 9.

77. *Yet the disdain* Twain wrote in "Jane Lampton Clemens," that "the 'nigger trader' was loathed by everybody." *HHT*, 49.

77. *from his home* Twain, "Jane Lampton Clemens," *HHT*, 51. For more on this incident see: *SCH*, 74–75; *Paine*, 1:43; Arthur G. Pettit, *Mark Twain and the South* (Lexington: University Press of Kentucky, 1974), 17–18.

77. *could not have the conscience* Twain, "Jane Lampton Clemens," *HHT*, 51.

78. *I knew the man had a right* Following the Equator, *OMT*, 352.

78. *Everybody seemed indifferent about it* Twain, typescript of notebook 28b, pp. 22–23, Mark Twain Papers; quoted in Pettit, *Mark Twain and the South*, 15.

78. *Everybody granted* The Tragedy of Pudd'nhead Wilson, *OMT*, 303.

78. *as a rule our slaves* Twain, "Jane Lampton Clemens," *HHT*, 49.

78. *Mistress always told us* Emma Knight, quoted in *The American Slave*, 203.

78. *Father run away.* Clay Smith, quoted in *The American Slave*, 263.

78. *loud and frequent groans* Paine, 1:17.

79. *In 1847, when Twain was eleven* Paine, 1:63–64; *SCH*, 148. The *Hannibal Journal* of Aug. 19, 1847, reported: "While some of our citizens were fishing a few days since on die Sny Island, they discovered in what is called Bird Slough the body of a negro man. On examination of the body, they found it to answer the description of a negro recently advertised in handbills as a runaway from Neriam

Todd, of Howard County. He had on a brown jeans frock coat, homemade linen pants, and a new pair of lined and bound shoes. The body when discovered was much mutilated." Quoted in *SCH*, 148.

79. *Indeed, slaves escaped HT*, 104.

79. *impressive pauses* Samuel Clemens to Joel Chandler Harris, Aug. 10, 1881; in *MTL*, 1: 402–3.

LYALL POWERS ON HUCK AS THE EMBODIMENT OF EMERSONIAN INDEPENDENCE

Associating Mark Twain with the term 'picaresque' will strike no reader as an original idea. Twain on several occasions conspicuously encouraged that association—or so it has seemed. But it has usually been a loose and perhaps irresponsible association, as it usually connects Twain and Cervantes. That in itself is acceptable enough: Cervantes' 'Exemplary Novel' *Rinconete and Cortadillo* (1613) is truly a picaresque tale of the adventures of two boys who are more than faintly anticipatory of Twain's famous pair, Tom and Huck.[1] It is not with this tale in mind, however, that the association is usually made, but with *Don Quixote*—and as a paradigm of 'picaresque'. A footnote in a popular 'critical edition' of *Adventures of Huckleberry Finn* is typical: it identifies Don Quixote as 'the "hero" of Cervantes' picaresque narrative (1605)'.[2] But perhaps that association and definition are not altogether red herrings, for they may encourage us to attempt to make distinctions that could prove useful: (1) to distinguish between *Don Quixote* and the true picaresque novel: (2) to see how that distinction might enable us to locate Twain's novels in a particular literary tradition; and (3) to discover how such a distinction can help clarify some problems in three of Twain's major works—*The Adventures of Tom Sawyer*, *Adventures of Huckleberry Finn*, and *A Connecticut Yankee in King Arthur's Court*.

The picaresque novel begins properly with the Spanish works *Lazarillo de Tormes* (1554) and *Guzman de Alfarache* (1599, 1604), and continues in such non-Spanish works as *Moll*

Flanders (1722), *Gil Blas* (1715, 1724, 1735), and *Roderick Random* (1748). The true picaresque novel is characterized by certain unmistakable features. It is the story of the peregrinations of a low-born hero, an alien obliged to live by his wits in order to survive in a hostile and hypocritical society. It is cast in the mould of autobiography, and thus involves a double time sequence—the time of the adventures recounted and the time of recounting them. That duality makes possible the moralizing implications of the autobiographer, particularly visible in *Guzman* and in the eighteenth-century, non-Spanish works. The dilemma of the picaro is that he must choose between conforming to the mores of the society in which he finds himself in order to survive, and adhering to what innate moral principles he may possess. Richard Bjornson aptly calls this dilemma the picaresque 'double-bind.'[3] The Spanish picaresque novel typically ends unhappily with the loss of the picaro to the pressure of social convention. The non-Spanish picaresque novels, on the other hand, typically end happily; the hero manages to remain true to the self and finally basks in the blessings of poetic justice.

(...)

Adventures of Huckleberry Finn exhibits most of the features of the true picaresque form. It is Huck's autobiography and thus has the typical dual-time sequence, although the distinction between the moment of the adventures and the moment of Huck's recording them is emphasized only in the concluding chapter. Huck is the outcast, still at bottom the alien even though. he has been momentarily accepted by society as the novel opens. His leaving first the Widow Douglas and then Pap initiates the expression of Huck's double-bind dilemma. Henceforth, Huck's adventures are quite the equivalent of the picaro's attempt to find a place in society. Whether or not the series of adventures ought properly to be called a 'quest', it clearly indicates that Huck is fleeing from a tyranny, represented by both the Widow and Pap, and is seeking a place in society where he can exist free of that tyranny. His goal, thus, is freedom—and is quite the equivalent of Jim's. One would not readily call Huck's struggle with society an ideological one; he is simply seeking—like the typical picaro from Lazarillo onward—the means to survive.

Huck's double-bind is likewise typical; the question is whether or not he will forsake his own integrity and become society's creature. He typically accepts the status quo; he tries to become what society wants, for every alias Huck assumes is tested for society's approval—the Duke and King tell him who he is to be, and the Phelpses finally tell him who he is. Huck occasionally comments that people can be awful cruel to each other, but any moral judgement he makes is against himself and made according to society's 'moral' standards. He is to that extent the victim of the socializing process, like Lazarillo de Tormes and Guzman de Alfarache. One sees evidence of this in the much discussed crucial scene (in Chapter XXXI) of Huck's decision not to turn in Jim—and the emphasis on the double-bind is quite apparent:

> It was a close place. I took it [the letter to Miss Watson] up, and held it in my hand. I was a-trembling, because I'd got to decide, forever, betwixt two things, and I knowed it. I studied a minute, sort of holding my breath, and then says to myself
> 'All right, then, I'll go to hell'—and tore it up.

That decision prepares exactly for Huck's final decision in the novel—to light out for the Territory.

Huck's story, like that of the typical Spanish picaro, ends unhappily. The difference is that while the Spanish picaro is finally victim of the socializing process and has surrendered whatever 'self' he began with, Huck is 'lost' because he cannot finally be false to himself. Huck's driving independence is truly Emersonian; he must abide by the voice within him (i.e., expressly *not* his conscience—the voice of *learned* duty), which he all too readily admits to be the voice of the Devil but is at last the only voice he knows. Huck's last decision is, then, essentially like that of Edna Pontellier in Kate Chopin's *The Awakening*; he sacrifices his physical self in order to maintain the freedom of his spiritual self.

The events that immediately lead up to and precipitate that final decision—beginning with the return of Tom to the scene of action—remind us that within the true picaresque form of *Adventures of Huckleberry Finn* is contained something of a quixotesque dialogue, with *Tom* as a kind of Don Quixote and Huck as Sancho Panza.[13] Here we find the persistence of the very dialogue that lies at the heart of *The Adventures of Tom Sawyer*, the only important difference is that Twain's sympathies have unmistakably shifted. And once again the aim is not to resolve the opposition between Tom and Huck by means of the quixotesque reciprocal modification, but to seek the victory of one of the two over the other. [T]he picaresque was fated to be modified by the genius of Cervantes into the masterpiece of Don Quixote.... There the dilemma [individual integrity versus social conformity] is not merely expressed but the resolution is artistically implied. Few have matched Cervantes' achievement; Twain did not, but his success in expressing the dilemma of the individual challenged by society is nonetheless an admirable enough achievement.

Notes

1. Harry Levin, in The Example of Cervantes' (1957), calls *Rinconete and Cortadillo* 'a tale endearing to American readers as a Sevillian adumbration of *Tom Sawyer* and *Huckleberry Finn*'; see *Cervantes: A Collection of Critical Essays*, ed. Lowry Nelson, Jr. (Englewood Cliffs, N.J.: Prentice-Hall, Inc., 1969), p. 41. See also Robert Giddings, *The Tradition of Smollett* (London: Methuen and Co. Ltd., 1967), p. 36: 'Many picaresque novelists are indebted to Cervantes, but to the Cervantes not of *Don Quixote* but *Rinconete y Cortadillo*.'

2. Norton Critical Edition of *Adventures of Huckleberry Finn*, ed. Sculley Bradley, Richmond Croom Beatty, E. Hudson Long and Thomas Cooley, 2nd ed. (New York: W.W. Norton and Co., Inc., 1977), p. 16.

3. *The Picaresque Hero in European Fiction* (Madison, Wisc.: University of Wisconsin Press, 1977), p. 11 and passim.

13. This is an 'inversion' of what we find in Cervantes' *Cipion and Berganza*; the apparently picaresque autobiography of Berganza is actually contained within the dialogue between Berganza and Cipion. See Aguinaga, ibid., p. 143.

JOHN E. BECKER ON THE WORK AS A SERIOUS NOVEL ADDRESSING CRITICAL SOCIAL ISSUES

Alienation

Unhappy with the culture that nourishes them, prophets prefer the outsider's stance. But the concept of the outsider is so familiar to us as "moderns" that it does not seem likely to serve us well in any attempt to define *prophecy*. We are all, if alienation is the keynote, prophets. And if we are all prophets, then *prophecy* includes so much it means nothing. Herbert N. Schneidau's "In Praise of Alienation" verifies this spontaneous recognition of our alienated selves, then tells us that, as a matter of fact, the alienated vision is paradoxically central to our culture.[1] It is, moreover, the result of habits of reflection taught us ultimately by the tradition of biblical prophecy. No matter how commonplace it is, then, alienation remains fundamental in any understanding of prophecy in literature.

If prophetic alienation is intrinsic to Western reflection, the task of sorting prophets from other verbal artists, or of distinguishing prophecy from other literature is, in some ways, futile. We must say from the beginning that prophecy is rather a dimension of literary expression than a genre. It may be discernible in many works that bear no clear resemblance to the types or forms of discourse that appear in the biblical books of prophecy.

(...)

Lying

Though Mark Twain may be an obvious choice for the role of prophet as we have been defining it, *The Adventures of Huckleberry Finn* may not at first blush seem an obvious choice as a book of prophecy. Still, it illustrates the concept of alienation well, and its theme—this is the contention of the reading that follows is most fundamentally concerned with the nature of truth. Establishing the credibility of the narrator and asserting his truth against the truths of culture is Twain's major effort. It may even be that the common critical complaint about the ending of the novel will seem less cogent if the reader adjusts his focus more sharply precisely on the issue of discovering truth.

Let us look first at the issue of language, an issue to which Twain draws our attention immediately, and in his own peculiar way. After warning us against taking the book seriously:

NOTICE

Persons attempting to find a motive in this narrative will be prosecuted; persons attempting to find a moral in it will be banished; persons attempting to find a plot in it will be shot.

BY ORDER OF THE AUTHOR
Per G.G., CHIEF OF ORDNANCE,

he immediately demands that we take its language very seriously:

EXPLANATORY

In this book a number of dialects are used, to wit: the Missouri negro dialect; the extremest form of the back-woods South-Western dialect; the ordinary "Pike-County" dialect; and four modified varieties of this last. The shadings have not been done in a haphazard fashion, or by guess-work; but painstakingly, and with the trustworthy guidance and support of personal familiarity with these several forms of speech.

I make this explanation for the reason that without it many readers would suppose that all these characters were trying to talk alike and not succeeding.

THE AUTHOR

It is easy enough to value the dramatic realism of dialect, along with the author's obvious pleasure both. in his own nostalgic memory and his artistic skill. But there is more than nostalgia here. The artistic risk is clear. Twain is abandoning the authority of a standard artistic style, a language that carries within its syntax and diction the authority of accepted literary high-seriousness; and the book, despite Twain's "Notice," is serious. Moreover, local dialects are historically ephemeral and geographically confined. Twain seems almost to be abandoning the hope of writing something that will touch many and that will last.

We may go further. Twain is dealing with racism,'a mode of perception so rooted in the ethos of Twain's world that it seemed altogether "natural." The language of that world, not excluding the literary language, embodies that racist ethos. Literature is not always prophetic; some of it, and sometimes almost all of it; may be concerned precisely with expressing the mythically based ethos of its particular form of oppression. Such literary language takes on the quality of ritual language, one of whose functions is to define and maintain the definition of just who "the people" are. An author who sets out to break down that definition and assert that a new definition is needed, a more inclusive definition, may have to burst the barriers of the accepted ritual language with a new, and newly authoritative vernacular speech.

Let me indicate what I mean, first with an example of what I consider a failed attempt, Bret Harte's attempt to show that even the wild men of the frontier were human. The few words spoken by the frontier characters in such stories as "Tennessee's Partner" are sentimental and unlikely. But the frontier actualities they are meant to convey are sapped of all credibility by the thick soup of condescension in the Latinate language of the narrators of these stories. The controlling voice remains the conventional voice of the oppressive majority. For all the stories of Bret Harte the frontiersman remains alien and unknown. Twain, on the other hand, inflicts a new and difficult language on his readers. It requires an unbending of the reader's mind, a willingness to let go of the authority of the conventional style associated with the serious issues and hear a new truth spoken out of the crude mouths of slaves and rootless boys. Twain, by the device of dialect, demands, as the prophets always demand, that we see these people on their own terms and in their own language. To those who are scandalized by the uncouth dialects of the frontier, where Twain received his revelation of truth, he says, "Hear ye, indeed, but understand not; and see ye indeed, but perceive not" (Isah. 6:9).

The frame of Twain's narrative, setting aside for a further moment the central drama of Huck and Jim, contains a virtual survey of the forms of cultural mythology. There is something almost systematic about this survey in the opening frame section of the narrative. It continues, however, after the dramatic relationship between Huck and Jim has been established, in the episodic excursions into the various worlds that live along the river bank, coming to a kind of climax in the elaborate efforts of the King and the Duke to steal the inheritance of the bereaved girls. The survey opens with some appropriate heavy-handed irony: Twain has Tom innocently identify respectability with membership in a band of robbers. It continues with a carefully orchestrated exposé of the various forms of religious mythology. Huck is presented with the story of Moses, but his pragmatic mind rejects taking any stock in dead people. The angel and harp version of heaven is given its due, an easy target. But Twain does not let Huck off either. He is as darkly pursued by irrational belief as any of his civilized teachers: gothic superstitions, ghosts, turning three times to make reparation for a burnt spider, a lock of hair to keep away witches. Jim belongs more to Huck's world than to the world of civilized superstition. His story explaining how his hat got lifted from his sleeping head and hung from the branch of a tree is simply a paradigm—Twain's paradigm, of course—for the growth of legends. Prayer gets its pragmatic test in chapter 3 and God's governance of the world is satirically split into two "Providences," the widow's and Miss Watson's.

But the careful balance of Twain's satire is clear from his next attack, which is on Tom's blind, secular faith in the authority of European fiction, namely, European norms of high culture. Tom is convinced that robbery and piracy are as strictly governed by convention, precedent, and rules as any aspect of civilized life. Such is the "romantic anarchy" he represents.

Note

1. Herbert Schneidau, *Sacred Discontent: The Bible and Western Tradition* (Berkeley: University of California Press, 1977), chap. 1. My debt to Schneidau is large but not exclusive. See my own "The Law, the Prophets, and Wisdom: On the Functions of Literature" (*College English* 37 (1975), pp. 254–64). It would appear that our thoughts have been independently running along the same lines.

Works by Mark Twain

The Celebrated Jumping Frog of Calaveras County, and Other Sketches, 1867.
The Innocents Abroad, 1869.
Mark Twain's Autobiography and First Romance, 1871.
Roughing It, 1872.
The Gilded Age, 1873.
Sketches New and Old, 1875.
Adventures of Tom Sawyer, 1876.
Old Times on the Mississippi, 1876.
A True Story and the Recent Carnival of Crime, 1877.
A Tramp Abroad, 1880.
The Prince and the Pauper, 1881.
The Stolen White Elephant, 1882.
Life on the Mississippi, 1883.
Adventures of Huckleberry Finn, 1884 (London); 1885 (American edition).
A Connecticut Yankee in King Arthur's Court, 1889.
The American Claimant, 1892.
The Tragedy of Puddn'head Wilson, 1894.
Tom Sawyer Abroad, Tom Sawyer Detective, and Other Stories, 1896.
How to Tell a Story and Other Essays, 1897.
Following the Equator; A Journey Around the World, 1897.
The Man That Corrupted Hadleyburg and Other Stories and Essays, 1900.
My Debut as a Literary Person, 1906.
What is Man?, 1906.
Is Shakespeare Dead?, 1909.

Annotated Bibliography

Beaver, Harold. *Huckleberry Finn*. London and Boston: Allen & Unwin, 1987.

Beaver discusses Huck's character as completely empirical, a detective with a keen eye for details and an acute sensibility to the world around him. Though Beaver sees Huck as given over to the pleasure principle, he is also endearing for his sensitivity. Most importantly, for Beaver, is Huck's loyalty to Tom, Jim, Pap, and even the king and duke.

Becker, John E. "Twain: The Statements Was Interesting but Tough" in *Poetic Prophecy in Western Literature*. Edited by Jan Wojcik and Raymond-Jean Frontain. Cranbury, New Jersey: Associated University Presses, 1984: 131–42.

Focusing on both theme and language, Becker maintains that Twain intended the reader to understand *Huckleberry Finn* as a serious book. Among other characteristics, Becker finds that Twain's utilization of highly realistic, local dialects can be construed as evidence that the author abandoned all hope of appealing to and being understood by a wide audience and, further, in his treatment of racism, Twain "inflicts a new and difficult language on his readers," so that they may hear a new truth spoken by disenfranchised slaves and homeless boys.

Bell, Millicent. "*Huckleberry Finn* and the Sleights of Imagination" in *One Hundred Years of Huckleberry Finn: The Boy, His Book and American Culture*. Edited by Robert Sattelmeyer and J. Donald Crowley. Columbia, Missouri: University of Missouri Press, 1985: 128–45.

While stating that *Huckleberry Finn* is a "modified frame story" in which Tom Sawyer is the dominant character, both in the beginning and final episodes of the novel, Bell discusses the important literary distinctions between them, namely that Huck's mind is fundamentally opposed to Tom's literary awareness, moral imagination and mode of speaking.

And, while *Huckleberry Finn* is rich in allusion, Bell nevertheless maintains that for all its humor and parody of literary conventions, *Huckleberry Finn* must be read as a serious expression of Twain's perspective on human life—in which individual identity is established "only by our willingness to accept definition of ourselves from the norms of society."

Budd, Louis J. "Introduction" to *New Essays on Adventures of Huckleberry Finn*. Edited by Louis J. Budd. Cambridge and New York: Cambridge University Press, 1985: 12–14.

Budd begins with a concise historical overview of *Huckleberry Finn* criticism from the 1890's through the early 1980's and focuses on those characteristics within the novel, and those critics who have acknowledged it as an American masterpiece deserving scholarly attention. Louis Budd's excellent introduction also discusses *Huckleberry Finn* from a biographical and historical context.

Carrington, George C., Jr. *The Dramatic Unity of "Huckleberry Finn."* Columbus, Ohio: Ohio State University Press, 1976: 120–24.

Carrington argues for a unity in *Huckleberry Finn* from a structuralist approach in which the critic allows "incidents and their effects [to] cluster into patterns" that lead to the emergence of a cohesive whole. Beginning with the premise that the disordered, topsy-turvy world of *Huckleberry Finn* and its narrator, who is incapable of discerning an implicit order hidden within the events he reports, Carrington maintains that both must be understood within the context of an inclusive system of "natural turbulence."

Egan, Michael. *Mark Twain's "Huckleberry Finn": Race, Class and Society*. London: Chatto & Windus Ltd. for Sussex University Press, 1977: 71–3

Citing differences in tone and characterization within the novel as evidence of the distress Twain felt when compelled to consider the social and political circumstances of the antebellum South that surround Huck and Jim's journey, Egan finds *Huckleberry Finn* to be one of the darkest novels in American literature. For a novel of incessant movement consumed with flight and escape, Egan maintains that *Huckleberry Finn* is essentially static in form and, further, fraught with tension because Twain felt obligated to provide a searing indictment of the antebellum South.

Emerson, Everett. "A New Voice for Samuel Clemens" in *The Authentic Mark Twain: A Literary Biography of Samuel L. Clemens.* Philadelphia: University of Pennsylvania Press, 1984: 127–50.

Emerson provides a biographical context for Twain's decision to make Huck the narrator and maintains that Huck's character provided Twain with a vehicle for expressing his own resistance and resentment for the "civilizing" he had to endure. In a word, Huck's celebration of self-indulgence and laziness, his pursuit of pleasure, and his caring for others allowed Twain to convey his authentic voice.

Everdell, William R. "Monologues of the Mad: Paris Cabaret and Modernist Narrative from Twain to Eliot." in *Studies in American Fiction* vol. 20, no. 2 (Autumn 1992): 177–196.

Citing Benjamin Franklin's autobiography as a precursor in its humor, informality and striving to achieve an emblematic truth, Everdell discusses *Huckleberry Finn* as a comic monologue which creates a bold immediacy in post-Romantic American literature. Characterizing Twain as a standup comic in his public lectures and appearances, with a fondness for telling anecdote and tall tales Everdell maintains that *Huckleberry Finn* is Twain's most honest work, written in his true voice.

Fiedler, Leslie. "*Huckleberry Finn*: Faust in the Eden of Childhood" in *Love and Death in the American Novel.* New York: Criterion Books (1960): 575–91.

Fielder identifies Huck's character as an American Faust—an independent spirit and a drifter—a sentimental version of the noble savage obsessed with death. He sees Huck as an adolescent boy born into a very dangerous world and forced to function on a sub-moral level, a reality which precipitates a crisis in which Huck's is forever caught between what he ought to do and what he must do. Nevertheless, though forced to accept his fate, Huck Finn retains a happy childish nature and the story ends with a burlesque treatment of its moral issues.

Krauth, Leland. "Southwestern Sentimentalist" in *Proper Mark Twain*. Athens and London: The University of Georgia Press, 1999: 166–88.

Krauth begins with a discussion of the relationship between *Life on the Mississippi River* and the genesis of *Huckleberry Finn*, with events chronicled in the former giving rise to Twain's creativity in the latter. Central to that imaginative reworking of his lived experiences is Twain's return to Hannibal in the spring of 1882, a return that is mixed with humor towards his boyhood memories and mourning for the now absent or deceased townspeople. Krauth situates *Huckleberry Finn* as belonging to both the literary tradition of Southwestern humor born of actual frontier life, class conflict and oral storytelling as well as an apologetic sentimentality and melodrama.

Gilman, Stephen. "*Adventures of Huckleberry Finn*: Experience of Samuel Clemens" in *One Hundred Years of Huckleberry Finn: The Boy, His Book, and American Culture*. Edited by Robert Sattelmeyer and J. Donald Crowley. Columbia: University of Missouri Press, 1985: 15–25.

Gilman discusses *Huckleberry Finn* in the context of Spanish picaresque novels, in particular those of his two contemporaries, Flaubert and Galdós. Gilman compares Huck's radical presence to that of "Christ for his disciples after the Crucifixion," both of whom remain after our reading of the text, and maintains that salvation of time" in *Huckleberry Finn* is exactly what differentiates it from picaresque narratives which represent the loss of *time*.

Gilman maintains that *Huckleberry Finn* is a profoundly historical novel as its themes of feuding, lynching and racial prejudice elucidate how the Civil War was possible.

McKay, Janet Holmgren. "'An Art so High': Style in *Adventures of Huckleberry Finn*" in *New Essays on Adventures of Huckleberry Finn*. Edited by Louis J. Budd. Cambridge and New York: Cambridge University Press, 1985: 61–81.

McKay focuses on the originality of style in *Huckleberry Finn* in the context of Twain's respect for the spoken word and his ability to work with all types of discourse, most especially his reverence for the "homely wisdom" contained in the vernacular. McKay's discusses Twain's literary achievement in having fashioned a narrator with the dual function of presenting a boy's innocence burdened with the perils of a social outcast.

Poirier, Richard. "Transatlantic Crossings: Mark Twain and Jane Austen" in *A World Elsewhere: The Place of Style in American Literature*. New York: Oxford University Press, 1966: 175–207.

Poirier compares Huck Finn to Jane Austen's protagonist, *Emma*, where both characters feign their identities for the sake of imitation or theatricality and, in so doing, renege on their respective social contracts. Unlike Emma, however, Poirier sees Huck's character as illustrative of a central problem of representation in American nineteenth-century fiction in which personal relationships are imagined within existing social environments. Poirier defines Huck's predicament as one in which his only viable form of self-expression is to constantly play "games" and tricks because "[t]here is no publicly accredited vocabulary which allows Huck to reveal his inner self to others.

Powers, Lyall. "Mark Twain and the Future of Picaresque" in *Mark Twain: A Sumptuous Variety*. Edited by Robert Giddings. London: Vision Press Limited and New York: Barnes & Noble Books, 1985: 155–175.

Powers focuses on the critical distinctions between the paradigm of the picaresque in Don Quixote and the "picaresque" characteristics in *Huckleberry Finn, Tom Sawyer* and *A Connecticut Yankee in King Arthur's Court*. With respect to Huck's character, Powers maintains that he is driven by an Emersonian independence, a need to be true to himself, rather than succumbing to the socializing process of the Spanish picaro. Among other things, Powers distinguishes Huck's compulsion for continued flight from "the rest" from the Cervantian compromise, which compulsion ultimately produces a tragic triumph in *Huckleberry Finn*.

Quirk, Tom. *Coming to Grips with "Huckleberry Finn": Essays on a Book, a Boy and a Man*. Columbia and London: University of Missouri Press, 1993.

A collection of Quirk's prior essays, this book focuses Twain's imaginative involvement with Huck Finn within the context of his autobiographical writings. Following a chronological survey of the novel's compositional stages, Quirk discusses *Huckleberry Finn's* relationship to nineteenth-century American realism, maintaining that there are two authors, Huck Finn and Mark Twain, existing in two distinct fictive worlds and, consequently, two different experiential realities—the "felt life" of Huck and the powerful satirical perspective of Twain's social commentary. Quirk's concluding chapters discuss "the patrimony of *Huckleberry Finn*" on such writers as Ring Lardner, Willa Cather and Langston Hughes, and, finally, its political correctness.

Rossky, William. *"The Reivers and Huckleberry Finn*: Faulkner and Twain." *The Huntington Library Quarterly* vol. XXVIII, no. 4 (August 1965): 373–376.

After pointing out many of the external resemblances between these two novels, Rossky focuses on the picaresque elements, what Orwell referred to as the "Sancho Panza aspect of life"—a revolt against rigid virtue, respectability, the pressures of time and the essential deadness of ordinary life. Rossky also sees Faulkner, and Twain to whom he is indebted, as offering a definition of what is uniquely "American" in the American novel, namely their respective portrayals of the "tramp" experience—a type far more complex than simply one who rejects the stifling forces of civilization.

Sloane, David E.E. *Adventures of Huckleberry Finn: American Comic Vision*. New York: Twayne Publishers, 1988.

Citing Twain's introductory disclaimer, in which he states that, among other things, he will shoot "plot-lovers," Sloane maintains that *Huckleberry Finn* begins with an obvious act of comic indirection in which the author doth protest too much. In identifying several compelling causes of action, motives and moral themes, Sloane maintains that Twain is consciously manipulating the reader, playing the part of the humorist in reverse as he provides a "a deadpan foreshadowing of the development of the novel's action."

Trilling, Lionel. "Huckleberry Finn" in *The Liberal Imagination: Essays on Literature and Society*. New York: Viking Press, 1950: 104–17.

Trilling declares *Huckleberry Finn* to be a great book containing the truth of moral passion, wherein Huck Finn's time on the Mississippi is likened to the service of a river-god which brings him close to an awareness of divinity of nature, a world replete with meaning in both natural signs and preternatural omens and taboos. Trilling sees Huck, who is at odds with natural religion, as experiencing the divine through the adoration he expresses and the homage he pays to the Mississippi as analogous to the chorus in a Greek tragedy singing a hymn of praise to the gods' beauty and mystery.

Walker. Nancy. "Reformers and Young Maidens: Women and Virtue in *Adventures of Huckleberry Finn*" in *One Hundred Years of* Huckleberry Finn: *The Boy, His Book, and American Culture*. Edited by Robert Sattelmeyer and

J. Donald Crowley. Columbia: University of Missouri Press, 1985: 171–185.

Walker discusses *Huckleberry Finn* as a thoroughly male novel. Narrated from the perspective of a young boy, it is a story of his passage from youthful innocence to maturity, with a desire to escape that is peculiarly both American and masculine. Walker's reading of *Huckleberry Finn* focuses on the basic tension between gender roles, which tension has a direct bearing on Huck's moral growth and in the end leads to a very limited maturity of his character.

Contributors

Harold Bloom is Sterling Professor of the Humanities at Yale University. He is the author of over 20 books, including *Shelley's Mythmaking* (1959), *The Visionary Company* (1961), *Blake's Apocalypse* (1963), *Yeats* (1970), *A Map of Misreading* (1975), *Kabbalah and Criticism* (1975), *Agon: Toward a Theory of Revisionism* (1982), *The American Religion* (1992), *The Western Canon* (1994), and *Omens of Millennium: The Gnosis of Angels, Dreams, and Resurrection* (1996). *The Anxiety of Influence* (1973) sets forth Professor Bloom's provocative theory of the literary relationships between the great writers and their predecessors. His most recent books include *Shakespeare: The Invention of the Human* (1998), a 1998 National Book Award finalist, *How to Read and Why* (2000), *Genius: A Mosaic of One Hundred Exemplary Creative Minds* (2002), *Hamlet: Poem Unlimited* (2003), and *Where Shall Wisdom be Found* (2004). In 1999, Professor Bloom received the prestigious American Academy of Arts and Letters Gold Medal for Criticism, and in 2002 he received the Catalonia International Prize.

Janyce Marson is a doctoral student at New York University. She is writing a dissertation on the rhetoric of the mechanical in Wordsworth, Coleridge, and Mary Shelley.

David E.E. Sloane has been Professor of English at the University of New Haven. He is the author of *Mark Twain as a Literary Comedian* (1979); *Sister Carrie: Theodore Dreiser's Sociological Tragedy* (1992) and editor of the *Student Companion to Mark Twain* (2001).

Louis J. Budd has been James B. Duke Professor and former chairman (1973–1979) of the Department of English at Duke University. He is the author of Our *Mark Twain: The Making of His Public Personality* (1983); *Robert Herrick* (1971); and a contributing editor of *The Gilded Age: A Tale of To-day/Mark Twain and Charles Dudley Warner* (2001).

Michael Egan is Professor of English at the University of Massachusetts at Amhearst. He is the author of *Extreme Situations: Literature and Crisis from the Great War to the Atom Bomb* (1979) and *Henry James: The Ibsen Years* (1972).

William R. Everdell's work has appeared in *Studies in American Fiction*.

Victor A. Doyno is a Professor at the State University of New York at Buffalo. He is the editor of *Mark Twain: Selected Writings of an American Skeptic* (1995) and *Parthenophil and Parthenophe* (1971).

Everett Emerson has been an Alumni Distinguished Professor in 1992 Professor and Professor Emeritus since 1993 at the University of North Carolina. He is the author of *Puritanism in America, 1620–1750* (1977); *The Authentic Mark Twain: A Literary Biography of Samuel L. Clemens* (1984); and editor of *Major Writers of Early American Literature* (1972).

George C. Carrington, Jr. has been a Professor of English at Northern Illinois University. He is the author of *The Immense Complex Drama: The World and Art of the Howells Novel* (1966) and co-author of *Plots and Characters in the Fiction of William Dean Howells* (1976).

Leland Krauth has been a Professor at the University of Colorado at Boulder. He is the author of *Mark Twain & Company: Six Literary Relations* (2003).

Richard Poirier has been a Professor at Rutgers University, New Brunswick, N.J. He is the author of *The Renewal of Literature: Emersonian Reflections* (1987); *Robert Frost: The Work of Knowing* (1990); and *Trying it Out in America: Literary and Other Performances* (1999).

Shelley Fisher Fishkin has been Professor of American Studies at the University of Texas in Austin. She is the author of *From*

Fact to Fiction: Journalism and Imaginative Writing in America (1985); *Was Huck Black?: Mark Twain and African-American Voices* (1993) an editor of *Listening to Silences: New Essays in Feminist Criticism* (1994).

Lyall Powers is the author of *Henry James and the Naturalist Movement* (1971); *"The Portrait of a Lady": Maiden, Woman, and Heroine* (1991); and *Alien Heart: The Life and Work of Margaret Laurence* (2003).

John E. Becker is Professor Emeritus of English, College at Florham Farleigh Dickinson University. He is the author of *Hawthorne's Historical Allegory: An Examination of the American Conscience* (1971) and other numerous articles on American literature.

Acknowledgments

Adventures of Huckleberry Finn: American Comic Vision by David E.E. Sloane. New York: Twayne Publishers (1988): 61–3. © 1988 by Twayne Publishers. Reprinted by permission of the Gale Group.

"Introduction" to *New Essays on Adventures of Huckleberry Finn* by Louis J. Budd Edited by Louis J. Budd. Cambridge and New York: Cambridge University Press (1985): 12–14. © 1985 by Cambridge University Press. Reprinted by permission of Cambridge University Press.

Mark Twain's "Huckleberry Finn": Race Class and Society by Michael Egan. London: Chatto & Windus Ltd. for Sussex University Press (1977): 71–3. © 1977 by Michael Egan. Reprinted by permission.

"Monologues of the Mad: Paris Cabaret and Modernist Narrative from Twain to Eliot" by William R. Everdell. *Studies in American Fiction* vol. 20, no. 2 (Autumn 1992): 177–8 and 183–4. © 1992 by Northeastern University. Reprinted by permission of Studies in American Fiction at Northeastern University.

Writing "Huck Finn": Mark Twain's Creative Process by Victor A. Doyno. Philadelphia: University of Pennsylvania Press (1991): 136–9. © 1991 by the University of Pennsylvania Press. Reprinted by permission of the University of Pennsylvania Press.

Mark Twain: A Literary Life by Everett Emerson. Philadelphia: University of Pennsylvania Press (2000): 150–2. © 2000 by Everett Emerson. Reprinted by permission of the University of Pennsylvania Press.

The Dramatic Unity of "Huckleberry Finn" by George C. Carrington, Jr. Columbus: Ohio State University Press (1976): 120–24. © 1976 by the Ohio State University Press; 1990 by Ildikó Carrington. Reprinted by permission of Ildikó Carrington.

Proper Mark Twain by Leland Krauth. Athens and London: The University of Georgia Press (1999): 172–4. © 1999 by the University of Georgia Press. Reprinted by permission.

"Transatlantic Crossings: Mark Twain and Jane Austen" by Richard Poirier. From *A World Elsewhere: The Place of Style in American Literature*. New York: Oxford University Press (1966): 147–50. © 1966 by Richard Poirier. Reprinted by permission of Oxford University Press, Inc.

Lighting Out for the Territory by Shelley Fisher Fishkin. New York and Oxford: Oxford University Press (1997): 19–22. © 1996 by Shelley Fisher Fishkin. Reprinted by permission of Oxford University Press, Inc.

"Mark Twain and the Future of Picaresque" by Lyall Powers. From *Mark Twain: A Sumptuous Variety*. Edited by Robert Giddings. London: Vision Press Limited and New York: Barnes & Noble Books (1985): 155–56 and 160–62. © 1985 by Vision Press Ltd. Reprinted by permission of the author.

"*Twain: The Statements Was Interesting but Tough*" by John E. Becker. From *Poetic Prophecy in Western Literature*. Edited by Jan Wojcik and Raymond-Jean Frontain. Cranbury, New Jersey (1984): 131 and 133–35. © 1984 by Associated University Presses, Inc. Reprinted by permission.

Index